The American South: A Very Short Introduction

VERY SHORT INTRODUCTIONS are for anyone wanting a stimulating and accessible way into a new subject. They are written by experts and have been translated into more than 45 different languages.

The series began in 1995, and now covers a wide variety of topics in every discipline. The VSI library currently contains over 650 volumes—a Very Short Introduction to everything from Psychology and Philosophy of Science to American History and Relativity—and continues to grow in every subject area.

Very Short Introductions available now:

ABOLITIONISM Richard S. Newman
THE ABRAHAMIC RELIGIONS
    Charles L. Cohen
ACCOUNTING Christopher Nobes
ADAM SMITH Christopher J. Berry
ADOLESCENCE Peter K. Smith
ADVERTISING Winston Fletcher
AERIAL WARFARE Frank Ledwidge
AESTHETICS Bence Nanay
AFRICAN AMERICAN RELIGION
    Eddie S. Glaude Jr
AFRICAN HISTORY John Parker and
    Richard Rathbone
AFRICAN POLITICS Ian Taylor
AFRICAN RELIGIONS
    Jacob K. Olupona
AGEING Nancy A. Pachana
AGNOSTICISM Robin Le Poidevin
AGRICULTURE Paul Brassley and
    Richard Soffe
ALBERT CAMUS Oliver Gloag
ALEXANDER THE GREAT
    Hugh Bowden
ALGEBRA Peter M. Higgins
AMERICAN BUSINESS HISTORY
    Walter A. Friedman
AMERICAN CULTURAL HISTORY
    Eric Avila
AMERICAN FOREIGN RELATIONS
    Andrew Preston
AMERICAN HISTORY Paul S. Boyer
AMERICAN IMMIGRATION
    David A. Gerber
AMERICAN LEGAL HISTORY
    G. Edward White

AMERICAN MILITARY HISTORY
    Joseph T. Glatthaar
AMERICAN NAVAL HISTORY
    Craig L. Symonds
AMERICAN POLITICAL HISTORY
    Donald Critchlow
AMERICAN POLITICAL PARTIES
    AND ELECTIONS L. Sandy Maisel
AMERICAN POLITICS Richard M. Valelly
THE AMERICAN PRESIDENCY
    Charles O. Jones
THE AMERICAN REVOLUTION
    Robert J. Allison
AMERICAN SLAVERY
    Heather Andrea Williams
THE AMERICAN SOUTH
    Charles Reagan Wilson
THE AMERICAN WEST Stephen Aron
AMERICAN WOMEN'S HISTORY
    Susan Ware
ANAESTHESIA Aidan O'Donnell
ANALYTIC PHILOSOPHY
    Michael Beaney
ANARCHISM Colin Ward
ANCIENT ASSYRIA Karen Radner
ANCIENT EGYPT Ian Shaw
ANCIENT EGYPTIAN ART AND
    ARCHITECTURE Christina Riggs
ANCIENT GREECE Paul Cartledge
THE ANCIENT NEAR EAST
    Amanda H. Podany
ANCIENT PHILOSOPHY Julia Annas
ANCIENT WARFARE
    Harry Sidebottom
ANGELS David Albert Jones

For more information visit our website

www.oup.com/vsi/

Charles Reagan Wilson

THE AMERICAN SOUTH

A Very Short Introduction

OXFORD
UNIVERSITY PRESS

OXFORD
UNIVERSITY PRESS

Oxford University Press is a department of the University of Oxford.
It furthers the University's objective of excellence in research, scholarship,
and education by publishing worldwide. Oxford is a registered trade mark of
Oxford University Press in the UK and certain other countries.

Published in the United States of America by Oxford University Press
198 Madison Avenue, New York, NY 10016, United States of America.

Library of Congress Cataloging-in-Publication Data

Names: Wilson, Charles Reagan, author.
Title: The American South : a very short introduction / Charles Reagan Wilson.
Description: [New York] : Oxford University Press, [2021] | Series:
Very short introductions | Includes bibliographical references and index.
Identifiers: LCCN 2020037968 | ISBN 9780199943517 (paperback) |
ISBN 9780199943579 (epub) | ISBN 9780199943562 (ebook)
Subjects: LCSH: Southern States—History. |
Southern States—Social life   and customs.
Classification: LCC F209 .W56 2021 | DDC 975—dc23
LC record available at https://lccn.loc.gov/2020037968

1 3 5 7 9 8 6 4 2

Printed in Great Britain by Ashford Colour Press Ltd., Gosport, Hants.,
on acid-free paper

Contents

Contents

List of illustrations

Introduction

The American South has a dramatic history that has made it a distinctive place on the world stage, one with continuing significance into the twenty-first century. Its early history illuminates the expansion of Europe into the New World, creating a colonial, plantation, slave society that made it different from other parts of the United States but fostered commonalities with other southern places that had similar colonial experiences. The Civil War and civil rights movement are historical events that transformed the South in differing ways and remain part of a vibrant public memory, one that the region's people and outsiders to the region often contest. In the twentieth century, the South's pronounced traditionalism in customs and values was in tension with the forces of modernization that only slowly forced change.

The American South has long evoked powerful imaginative responses to these experiences, making it well known around the world through films, literature, and music. Writers probe the psychology of its people, and scholars analyze its culture. Travelers sketch their observations on the customs of the people they meet, and southerners themselves brood over their inheritance and their destiny. Country ballads and blues music lay bare the South's complexities and tragedies but celebrate the joy of life in the region as well. The cultures that took root in the South grew out of physiographic locales and ecologies and the differing ethnic backgrounds of people who shaped the land and its human societies. Two broad geographical subdivisions anchor what became known as "the South"—an Uplands, stretching from the Appalachian Mountains in the eastern South through the hill country of Kentucky, Tennessee, Arkansas, and into central Texas; and a Lowlands, from the Atlantic coast through the Gulf South, the Piney Woods, and the Deep South of the Black Belt and the Mississippi Delta.

Several themes shape this narrative introduction to the South. One is an inevitable concern with what has made the region different from other American places. Pervasive southern storytelling and American stereotyping have highlighted the South's places and peoples as different from those elsewhere in the nation. Despite dramatic convergences of the South with the rest of the nation, public opinion polling and other evidence suggests southerners and nonsoutherners still identify such traits as not only manners and hospitality, but also violence and prejudice with the South. A second theme is the one scholars increasingly stress—that the South exemplifies, sometimes in the extreme, American experiences. A third theme now places the South into an even broader context than the North–South one, namely, a global perspective that shows long-standing southern connections with the Atlantic world, especially the Caribbean islands. Much of the South's history was that of a colonial society, and its people still struggle with its aftermath as a postcolonial society. A fourth theme is the centrality of cultures in understanding the ideological, material, and spiritual experiences of people in the region. Promoters of southern unity have always stressed the singularity of its culture, but in fact, many cultures have grown out of the productive southern soil. Finally, southern life has always had a multicultural nature. Although racial concerns have been at the center of American life in general, no other place has engaged people of such differing backgrounds as western Europeans and West Africans over such a long period of time. The region's whites tried to segregate the races, but they could not segregate the eardrum, the eye, or the palate, so that the vibrant music, art, and food that have come out of the South show a cultural interaction, despite formal separation of racial groups. The South has now become the new center of immigration, adding to the complexity of the region's life as it emerges into a new twenty-first-century demographic complexity.

Recent scholarship has expanded the time frames of southern history, going back in time beyond the early nineteenth-century sectional conflict that promoted a more pronounced regional consciousness. The indigenous tribes of the Southeast were the first creators of southern places, and their legacy long outlived their exile to the Southwest. The colonial-era South now appears as the most heterogenous part of North America, given the variety of European and African peoples who came there. Historians are breaking down the borders of the South to focus on regions within the larger South and to explore border areas, as well as core zones of southern cultural life. The region's dominant public culture, expressed in officially sanctioned rituals and narratives that established authorized versions of the past while ignoring the experiences of minority groups, was part of the exercise of power by some southerners over others. Folkways that grew out of the interaction of Native Americans and peoples from western Europe and West Africa, within the context of a predominantly agricultural economy and rural life, give glimpses of a grass-roots South sometimes in opposition to the public culture.

Speaking of the South brings attention to the importance of regionalism in American history. The vast scale of American geography and adaptation of human cultures to their environments promoted the emergence and development of regional cultures. The larger areas—the South, the West, New England, and the Midwest—have massive scholarship documenting them, with those places each playing differing roles in the nation. Within the American South, a plethora of regions—the Mississippi delta, south Louisiana, the bluegrass, the hill

3

country, the Piedmont, the tidewater, the Appalachians, and the Ozarks, among others—bring the abstract descriptor of the South down to the ground of localism. The "spatial" turn in cultural studies is apparent in looking at the history of the American South.

Commentators on the South sometimes call Atlanta its capital, and anyone from the region flying elsewhere through the busy and crowded Hartsfield–Jackson Atlanta International Airport would recognize its centrality to the region at least. You cannot get to heaven, the saying goes, without going through Atlanta. Transportation and communication have always defined the city, from its beginnings in the 1830s as a remote transportation outpost named Terminus, to the role of super–television station WTBS in the 1970s, to housing the busiest airport in the world. Known as the Gateway City of the South in the nineteenth century and the City Too Busy to Hate in the 1950s and 1960s, Atlanta now promotes itself as the World's Next Great City.

The Georgia capital hosted the 1996 Olympics, arguably the moment when Atlanta, and the South, took a giant leap onto the contemporary world stage. To be sure, global movie audiences had watched the burning of Atlanta during the Civil War in *Gone with the Wind* (1939), the story of military defeat and occupation touching audiences in many places in the World War II era; and the world recognized that the civil rights movement was part of a worldwide freedom struggle by twentieth-century people of color. But the Olympics is one of the most prominent international events, and winning the right to host it was an undeniable boon to a perpetually boom-oriented city.

In its proposal to the International Olympic Committee, the city highlighted the American South's racial progress since the civil rights movement, with Mayor Andrew Young—one of the most prominent civil rights leaders—able to speak with authority to that point. Boosting the local economy through tourism and

4

economic development was a major goal of Atlanta's Olympic leaders, who hoped to use the occasion to gather money for infrastructure improvements and the remaking of downtown Atlanta, which had suffered from the flight of middle- and upper-class whites to the suburbs since the 1970s.

The Olympic programs highlighted southern cultural images, from soul singer Gladys Knight singing "Georgia on My Mind" (the state song) at the opening ceremonies to a "Welcome to the World" feature that celebrated a college football Saturday in the South, with cheerleaders, Chevrolet pickup trucks, marching bands, and high steppers from African American football tradition. Another feature, "Summertime," showcased Atlanta and southern history, culture, music, spirit, and the city's rebuilding after the Civil War.

The logistical challenges of the Atlanta games proved embarrassing for such a future-oriented city. And then a terrorist attack by a lone gunman brought anxiety to athletes and others attending. All this took some of the glow off the glittering hopes of the Olympics organizers to present the city and its region with undiluted glory.

Atlanta could brag about the estimated $5.41 billion economic impact, 2 million visitors for the games, and 3.5 billion viewers on televisions around the world. Modern infrastructure improvements included dormitories built for the games converted to Georgia Tech University housing, construction of multiple athletic facilities, improvements to two housing projects, upgrades to the sewer system, repair of dilapidated bridges, and the lasting memorial of the games—Centennial Stadium, which became the home of the city's Major League Baseball team, the Braves.

The Atlanta games refurbished the South's claim to a special southern hospitality (through relentless mentioning of it), but the complex issues of southern race relations were hard for visitors to miss. That mid-1990s moment saw escalating controversies about public display of the Confederate flag, especially the appearance of the flag's defining image—St. Andrew's Cross—on the Georgia state flag. African Americans saw the image as a throwback to slavery and racial segregation, while some whites believed it represented the heritage of a region that had experienced, and should not forget, the historical traumas of Civil War defeat. The well-promoted ideal of racial harmony, which had been a dream of southern commercial advocates since the New South movement led by Atlanta newspaper editor Henry Grady in the 1880s, was contradicted by the controversial monument at Stone Mountain, only a short drive from Atlanta, with the images of three Confederate heroes carved into a giant stone outcropping.

The Atlanta Olympics epitomizes such themes as race relations, economic development, and cultural expression that figure prominently in the larger story of the American South. It dramatized for international audiences that, despite all the changes in the region since the 1960s, its biggest city remained a vital place. The South matters as a meeting place of peoples from Europe and Africa who interacted with indigenous peoples to create a fractious but creative place. Along the way, a southern identity evolved, but it has remained a recognizable one. The screenwriter and actor Eugene Walter, born in Mobile, Alabama, who collaborated on many films with Federico Fellini, wrote in 1971, "when I say, 'I'm Southern'—most people, even in Europe, know what is signified." They knew that he came from "that country within a country, recognized as such although having no definable boundary." On his terrace above a busy street in Rome, he grew mint for his mint juleps and wormwood in case he wanted to make absinthe—tokens of a regional identity he could embody from Mobile to Rome.

Chapter 1
Becoming southern

Native peoples became the first southerners. Although they would not have used that descriptor, they developed the first regional culture from environmental conditions that would always be a foundation of regional life. A shared symbolism crossed a region from Texas to the Atlantic Ocean and from the Ohio River valley into Florida, including origin stories that typically represented native peoples emerging out of a world covered with water, as with a crawfish in Louisiana diving to the bottom and bringing up the mud that became dry land. Winged serpents and birdlike human warriors enlivened imaginations, while a mythic cross represented the earth and its cardinal directions. A robust trade in finished crafts took Etowah copper carvings throughout the region, and the temple mound at Cahokia in present-day Missouri displayed carved shells from the Atlantic and suggested a western limit to this first South.

In the early thirteenth century, the culture of the Mississippian period declined, with the depletion of timber and game, chronic tribal warfare, and loss of population. Southeastern tribes adapted and reorganized. The arrival of Europeans beginning in the fifteenth century challenged Native Americans of the Southeast, and new diseases and warfare contributed to the area becoming a "shatter zone" that resulted in their decline. Native groups formed new tribes. By the mid-1700s, Indians were no longer effectively challenging white authority in Virginia and the Carolinas, but in the interior and border areas, the Indian population was twice as large as the combined white/black population. Still, an estimated population decline of as much as 70 percent between 1500 and 1600 and another third in the eighteenth century decimated native life.

European settlement

The Europeans who came to the southeastern area of North America, what became the American South, brought with them preconceptions about that area, which was part of a New World that evoked images of a tropical climate, of fertile land that produced staple crops to enrich European nations, but also represented exploitation of African and indigenous labor and the threat of racial intermingling. If the Puritans established New England as a city on a hill, the white colonists in southern areas drew from earlier European imagery in portraying their region as a southern paradise. The English adventurer Sir Walter Raleigh had predicted that the Garden of Eden would be found in the New World on the thirty-fifth parallel of latitude—on a line now between Fayetteville, North Carolina, and Memphis, Tennessee.

There was a recurring religious dimension to the images of the southern colonies, which Europeans described as a "land of Canaan" and "a promised land." One of the first texts to interpret the emergent South was Robert Beverley's *The History and Present State of Virginia* (1705), which developed the image of the Virginia plantation as a paradise, an Arcadia as in classical times, with all the positive implications of that heritage. He confronted as well the special circumstances of slaves in the garden, foreshadowing the efforts of nineteenth-century southern writers to see how a paradise could contain African slaves.

Before the English came to Virginia, Spanish and French explorers were the leading edge of European incursions into

Indian lands of the South. Lucas Vazquez de Ayllon insisted in 1521 that he had found a new land, along the Gulf Coast, on the same latitude as the province of Andalusia in Spain. It was a place of abundance that could produce olive oil and wine, which was bound to get a Spaniard's attention. The Spanish went thus to Florida, and Hernando de Soto landed at Bradenton in 1539, exploring the South to the Mississippi River and leaving a bloody trail, enslaved indigenous people, and disease. De Soto's death and burial in the Mississippi River was a cautionary tale of early exploration in search of European dreams in the South. In the 1560s, the Spanish founded St. Augustine, the first European settlement in the southeastern part of North America. France undertook European development of the Mississippi River valley through early explorations from the north and by founding the colony of Louisiana in 1699.

Jamestown in Virginia was the first successful English colony, established in 1607, and other southern colonies followed. The climate in these places favored a long growing season and promoted an agricultural economy based on tobacco, rice, and indigo, and later, cotton and sugar. Contemporary observers saw that architecture, clothing, and even the pace of life and speech were affected by a climate that supposedly produced a characteristic lethargy and gave birth to a tenacious stereotype of southern laziness. Geography did not, however, unify the emergent South. Mountain ranges and rivers divide the South, and its plains and valleys run north and south, connecting with land in other regions. Mountains and hill country areas, for example, were favored by small-scale yeoman farmers, while the lowlands were home to wealthy plantation owners and enslaved peoples.

The eighteenth century

The early 1700s were crucial years in the emergent South. The population grew, the colonial economy and society matured, planter elites asserted colonial political power within the empire, and colonists relied increasingly on chattel slavery of Africans. The accumulation of land by the early 1700s enabled a few planters to gain cultural authority within an increasingly hierarchical world of gentlemen and their women, slaves, and yeoman farmers. The plantation mansion became perhaps the earliest symbol of an emerging southern identity in the eighteenth century.

Anglicanism, an American version of the English national religion, was the established church in the southern colonies, and it provided a degree of unity through worship services, a common theology and moral values, and education. The English country gentleman ideal was transplanted to the southern colonies by the 1700s. Pastoral imagery of settled farms and livestock herding that harked back to Arcadian images of classical civilization became the model for the emergent southern elite.

Out of a self-conscious cultural identity crisis of the early 1700s, as colonists began to grapple with their situation far from the home country of England, came new loyalties to colonial identities and a broader sense of regional community based in shared social arrangements. Virginian William Byrd II was a representative figure in the adaptation of the English gentry identity to an evolving southern context. Born in England, he became a self-conscious Virginian and a model for later southern planters. He saw financial matters as central concerns to New England merchants and slave traders and believed his slave-owner class was different from them in attention to an ethic of honor and religious values. He foresaw bad consequences from the growing numbers of African slaves in Virginia, who were increasing so rapidly that he feared the colony would soon go by the "Name of New Guinea." Byrd devoted most of his extensive writings, however, to separating himself from the plain white folk. His account of surveying the dividing line between North Carolina and Virginia identified the differences between his "people" and

1. This painting from the early national period depicts both the natural world and the household of southern slave society. A hunter from a well-off family returns with a fowl, greeted by a white child and, likely, his African American domestic servant. The artist was untrained but used clothing, the natural setting, and the enslaved servant to suggest the family's privileged status.

the frontier plain whites. Byrd sketched a lively, but troubling to him, image of "Lubberland," a frontier wasteland in Carolina. Wealthy planters had gradually gained control of the best Virginia lands in the sixteenth century, leaving poorer sorts frustrated. In Bacon's Rebellion (1679), Nathaniel Bacon, a young English gentleman only recently arrived in the colony, organized frontier planters to oppose larger planter families who controlled the colonial government. The frontier planters favored a harsh Indian policy to secure their landholdings, but Governor William Berkeley used the militia to subdue the rebellion and augment the authority of the largest planter estates.

White racial dominance emerged as soon as Europeans, Indians, and Africans met each other in the early days of Virginia. A Dutch ship brought twenty Africans to Jamestown in 1619, the very year that Virginia established the House of Burgesses to govern the colony, symbolizing the promise of political liberty. The slave population expanded throughout the southern colonies in the late 1600s and early 1700s, bringing wealth to white landowners but stoking whites' fear of black people in their midst. The Stono Rebellion (1739) in South Carolina was a slave insurrection that led to the deaths of about twenty-five white people and thirty-five enslaved people. It brought more regulation of slave life and pressures to end the slave trade. The triangular trade between the Caribbean, New England, and the South brought wealth to the colonies, and European and African cultures were surely formative ones in the South. Southern planters raised staple crops to market in the emerging capitalist world system. The commodification of African bodies was a terrible symbol of the dark side of transatlantic connections, but black people became an active influence in a nascent creolized southern society.

Cultural foundations

The history of the South properly begins with Native Americans whose use of natural resources and their location of settlements and transportation routes would be models for Europeans and Africans. Indian names still mark rivers and states, and their agricultural and dietary habits linger as later southerners eat grits and squash casseroles. Likewise, the folk medicine passed down across generations of southerners is a mixture of Indian herbal knowledge and European and African elements. Many of the folk tales in southern oral tradition are originally from Native American lore. European influence was apparent as well. The British social class structure, European musical and literary forms, Enlightenment rationalism, Christian theologies and institutions, and European farming techniques all became vital, evolving elements of early southern culture as well.

Africans contributed specific knowledge from their homelands, as their familiarity with herding livestock and cultivating rice and indigo enriched the early Carolina Lowcountry. Despite the rigid legal boundaries of an emerging caste system, cultural integration began through the transfer of knowledge, customs, and ways of separate peoples. The years between 1720 and 1780 were a cultural watershed for black southerners because importation of slaves dramatically increased. Slaves from different African regions and tribal origins used pidgin languages to forge new identities in the South. Slaves remembered and passed along African ideas about family, the individual's place in the universe, musical forms, and skills such as metalworking and wood carving, herding, boat making and navigation, and rice cultivation. Slaves devised long-lasting traditions of rhythmic music and dance and of communal child raising. The slave quarters were a hearthstone for an African American version of southern culture.

The frontier experience also shaped the emergence of a southern identity. As settlers moved west, conflicts developed between the tidewater gentry and the backcountry yeomen, often class conflicts that mirrored social divisions between eastern and western parts of the southern colonies. New ethnic populations put their mark on the frontier as well. Scots-Irish and German settlers came to North America in increasing numbers in the mid-1700s, and they migrated from western Pennsylvania into the Piedmont and soon crossed the Appalachian Mountains. The Scots-Irish represented an especially large ethnic culture introduced into southern life in the colonial era, one that became associated with the frontier. If the tidewater aristocracy was English in style and outlook, the Scots-Irish left their imprint to the west. Their ballad-singing musical forms became one basis for later country music singers. They planted Calvinist religious ideas that would feed into the South's predominant evangelical Protestant faith. They became self-sufficient farmers and practiced herding techniques brought from their northern Ireland homelands. Colonists from Germany, Switzerland, the

Netherlands, France, Scotland, and Ireland joined with the larger numbers of English and Africans, often mixing together in the backcountry.

The American Revolution

The American Revolutionary era (1775–89) was a landmark in the appearance of a self-conscious southern identity. One historian has called these years the "First South," a place geographically defined with a western boundary at the Mississippi River, stable communities along the Atlantic coast, and interior lands still mostly occupied by native groups. Charles Mason and Jeremiah Dixon drew their surveyor's line between Pennsylvania and Maryland in the 1760s, but they did so to settle a boundary dispute between the colonies without the intention of demarking a "North" and "South." The Ohio River and the Mason–Dixon line, however, became symbolic dividers between new states. The first census, in 1790, revealed roughly equal population settlement both north and south of that line, documenting 1.9 million people (over a third of whom were African American) south of the line and 2 million north of it.

The Revolutionary War gave the colonists a common enemy, but other unifying forces had developed over the course of their nearly two centuries living in North America, including their shared English language, a mostly western European inheritance among colonists (with the important exception of slaves), an appreciation of self-governance, and transportation, communication, and trade relationships across the colonies. White southerners were central figures in the drama of the Revolution, from taking an active role in the First Continental Congress in 1774 to serving in Virginian George Washington's presidential administration in the 1790s. Nationalism triumphed, but it provided a new context for the recognition of sectionalist concerns within the new union. The differing interests of northern and southern colonists brought strife to the First Continental Congress, for example, and southern planters feared northern mercantile dominance at the Philadelphia Convention that created the Constitution in 1787. Conflicts emerged there and in the new federal government over regional interests, especially those related to trade and to the protection of slavery.

White southerners became aware of their dilemma as slave owners in a democratic republic and thereby helped to promote regional self-consciousness. The debate over slavery during the Philadelphia Convention in 1787 (and its three-fifths compromise, which counted slaves as three-fifths human) dramatized white southerners' recognition of their racial situation and its political meanings. The slave uprising in St. Domingo in the early 1790s and Gabriel Prosser's slave conspiracy near Richmond in 1800 compelled whites to think about the slaves in their midst as potential rebels.

Sectional feelings had existed during the colonial era, but they took new shape in the early national period to 1830. White southerners saw New Englanders as self-righteous moralists, while northern travelers and newspapers painted white southerners as lazy, given to brawling, and too fond of whiskey. One northern writer judged white southerners as "slingers," who used a sling of whiskey to start their days. Noah Webster, the Massachusetts scholar who would help define an American language, disliked the southerners he had met, but he agreed nonetheless to give lectures in Virginia. He concluded that the people he met had a "great fondness for dissipated life." This wordsmith went further and noted that "they do not understand grammar." It was an ugly charge, indeed.

The early national South

The growth of the frontier after the War of 1812 led to the appearance of regional stereotypes, as did the spread of a democratic ideology. Such egalitarian ideals as natural rights, popular sovereignty, contractual government, and human perfectibility took root in the South in the new state constitutions written after the Revolution and into the 1820s. Patterns of voting and political behavior in the southern states, in general, continued nonetheless to be beholden to deference, tradition, and the social structure that invested authority in elites. Rhetorical democracy was a triumph for the plain white folk, however, at times enabling them to challenge the dominance of the planter class.

Religious changes in the Jeffersonian-era South interacted with the rise of democratic forces that brought the plain folk into greater prominence there. The rise of evangelical Protestant groups—the Methodists, Baptists, and Presbyterians—brought a passionate new spiritual force to the region. The Great Revival of 1800–1805 was one of the turning points in southern cultural history, because it marked the emergence of evangelicalism as a formative force on the region's character. Evangelicals appeared in the southern colonies in the mid-eighteenth century as dissenters and even social outcasts. The Baptist counterculture at the time embodied the spirit of a radical egalitarianism that championed the ideals of religious freedom, the brotherhood of man, and the nurturing community of the saved. Evangelicals at first encouraged black converts, women prophets, and young male itinerant preachers. At times, blacks and whites worshiped together, albeit in segregated seating, and many evangelicals as late as the early national period questioned the institution of slavery.

Evangelicals in the early decades of the nineteenth century made their peace, however, with a southern culture dominated by racist, paternalistic, and patriarchal values. Their primary aim all along had been to preach the gospel as a way to salvation, and they came to believe that questioning the dominant social patterns of southern society was hampering their mission. They thus compromised on the emancipation of slaves, the spiritual empowerment of women, and reliance on young charismatic preachers to deliver their message in peace to the slaves as well as to whites. By 1830, the Methodists, Baptists, and Presbyterians had become numerically and culturally prominent in the South.

Racial fears remained a part of the white psyche in a biracial society. Slavery was not dying out, because Eli Whitney's invention of the cotton gin in 1793 enabled planters to expand their properties that still depended on slave labor. It was a profitable system for most slave owners, and their privileged lifestyles relied on it. For whites who were not slave owners or owned only a few slaves, social success nonetheless depended on slaves and land. Moreover, the thought of slavery's abolition suggested the possibility of equality of black people and white, an unthinkable proposition for most of the latter. Jefferson's dream of a republic of free people was for whites only. He fathered a child by his slave, Sally Hemings, and his own intimate relationship with her symbolized the complex segregation and connection of southern white and black people in an evolving slave society.

Jefferson championed the revolutionary ideas of liberty, freedom, equality of opportunity, and democracy that helped to establish the American liberal tradition. His vision rested in agrarian thought, lauding the self-sufficient agricultural life, harking back to classical images of virtue, and serving as a continuing southern-based critique of the greedy commercialism that American capitalism represented to many Americans. Jefferson saw expansion into the West as important for the spread of democracy, and his willingness to support the Louisiana Purchase in 1803 indeed spread agrarianism into new lands. By the 1840s, however, white southerners were emphasizing another element of Jefferson's vision—states' rights politics and the limitations on the use of federal power that he advocated.

The first few decades of the nineteenth century saw an economic transformation in the new southern states. The spread of the cotton gin, the emergence of sugar growing in Louisiana in the mid-1790s, the steady movement of whites after the War of 1812 into southeastern Indian lands of the interior South, and the rising prices for frontier lands in the early 1800s brought increased reliance on agricultural staple crops. Elite families owned most of the best lands and were accumulating outlandish profits, as cotton became the powerful symbol of the region's expansive growth into the Old Southwest.

The career of Andrew Jackson epitomizes the emergence of a southern consciousness that was still in the making by 1830. Born in upland South Carolina of Scots-Irish ancestry, he moved to frontier Tennessee at age nineteen, always seeing himself as a westerner and an American more than a southerner. He nonetheless held considerable land near Nashville, owned slaves, and lived as a gentleman patrician in a mansion he named The Hermitage. Jackson helped form the Democratic Party to compete with the Whigs, thus establishing the two-party system. Jackson's party drew from Jefferson's agrarian and democratic ideology; it was loyal to the Union and strict construction of the US Constitution, which the party's slave-owning constituency long used for protection against rising abolitionism after 1830. Yeoman farmers, in the South and elsewhere, could easily see themselves in Jackson and remained a key part of his coalition, as did many northern and midwestern working-class people.

The Jacksonians lived through the expansion of the market economy after the War of 1812, suspicious of the special privileges that economic and political elites had, privileges that threatened the liberties of plain people. Jackson and his party opposed Whig programs to fund and support economic development, financial maneuverings, protective tariffs, public schools, and progressive societal reform measures, while they supported limited government and minimal taxation, ideas rooted on the frontier but tenaciously surviving throughout southern history.

2. In 1821, the Cherokee leader Sequoyah devised the Cherokee alphabet, a landmark in the development of a Native American written language and a symbol of Indian movement toward the mainstream of American culture. The forced Cherokee removal to the West took place, nonetheless, in the 1830s, but the alphabet enabled the western natives to keep in touch with those Cherokees who had managed to stay behind in North Carolina, Georgia, and Tennessee.

Jackson oversaw one of the most tragic aspects of southern history—the expulsion of Native Americans from their ancestral lands in the Southeast. Beginning in George Washington's administration, the federal government's policy had tried to provide resources to help natives adapt to white ways and become "civilized." Indian agents and Protestant missionaries became emissaries to the Five Civilized Tribes—the Cherokees, Creeks, Chickasaws, Choctaws, and Seminoles. They insisted that natives obey written laws, that they respect individual property rights, that males farm and women weave European-style clothing, and that children attend school and learn the value of money and the Bible. The Five Civilized Tribes found social and economic models in nearby planters in the Southeast because plantations, staple crops, and slaves represented success there. As much as 10 percent of the population living in the Cherokee Nation in the mid-1820s consisted of African American slaves. The Cherokees went further than other tribes down the path of assimilation to white norms; in 1827 they adopted a constitution modeled after the US Constitution.

The relentless pressure of whites moving into the Deep South brought political pressure to remove the native tribes, with Andrew Jackson leading the way. Intimidation and violence led most of the southern tribes to sell their lands in exchange for territory in the West by the 1920s, but the Cherokees fought removal through legal and political efforts. Jackson justified the forced removal of the Cherokees as a necessity for economic development and to prevent the total elimination of natives that might result if they remained in contact with whites. Cherokee leaders understood that whites now saw the issue as one not of culture but of race, departing from the earlier Enlightenment understanding that Indians could become civilized. Hardening racial views in the 1830s led whites to categorize natives as racially inferior and impossible to incorporate into white-dominated society. The Trail of Tears, the melancholy descriptor of the natives' march to Indian Territory west of the Mississippi River, causing thousands of deaths, is a sobering marker of southern society's early commitment to white dominance and the expansion of the Cotton Kingdom at any cost. White southerners became southern at the expense of the indigenous people of the Southeast.

Chapter 2
Section to nation

By 1830, the South had long had a predominantly agricultural economy, and its people soon idealized the agrarian republic that had taken shape after the Revolution as the basis for an emerging sectional identity. To be sure, recent scholarship emphasizes that aspects of modernity had touched the pre–Civil War South. Southern coastal cities tied the broader South to international economic and intellectual currents, and inland cities functioned as suppliers and processors for the surrounding countryside. Industrialization had taken root in parts of the South, creating a more diverse economy than one might expect, and railroads connected some of the larger cities. Immigration brought change, as the Irish, for example, entered the region's workforce, especially in coastal cities. Still, the North changed far more than the southern states between 1830 and 1860. Market forces brought capitalism front and center to northern areas, while the South remained overwhelmingly agricultural in economy and rural in settlement.

Many apparent differences appeared between what had come to be called "the South" and other American places: the South was overwhelmingly rural in its population settlement compared to the exploding growth of northern cities; wealth rested in agricultural products in the South rather than the prosperity coming from expanding industrialization in the North; African

Americans and whites both had long genealogies in the South compared with a northern society that included more people of recent European background. However, one might also point out similarities between these American places, including speaking the same language, accepting English common law, embracing the Revolutionary legacy, honoring private property, and worshipping mostly in Protestant churches.

Whatever the mix of similarities and differences, efforts to construct a southern identity in the antebellum era appeared in the spread of sectional terminology. By 1830, when political sectionalism heightened, such terms as *South* and *Southland*, which related to the geographical region, were in widespread use in the United States. Americans commonly compared *the* southern place to other American places in travel accounts, newspaper stories, minstrel shows, and fiction. Between 1830 and 1860, some thirty periodicals used *southern* in their titles, whereas the word had seldom been used earlier. Such terms as *southerner* and *southron*, relating to the identity of whites in the region, became common after 1830, and the terms came to evoke moral meanings, positive for some people, negative for others.

The southern identity of the antebellum era reflected the attitudes of an agrarian republic. Localism loomed large in southern regional life. People lived on widely scattered small farms and plantations. Travelers complained of terrible roads, which worked to reinforce localistic orientations, because it was difficult to get anywhere. Everyday life focused on experiences with nearby places and people—the household, a few neighbors, the local congregation, the crossroads store, and the county seat. "Visiting" was a well-established tradition, sometimes an all-day affair or longer, because the difficulty of travel made it worthwhile to "stay a little longer," as the country song later noted.

Staple-crop agriculture typified the region as a whole, although the exhausted tobacco-growing soils of the seaboard South could not compete in productivity by the 1830s with the newly opened lands in the Old Southwest. Cotton now became the great money crop, tying the region called the South together and honored as "King Cotton." But corn was even more important in some ways to the region's agricultural life, because most everyone on farms grew it for table food and for their livestock. A complex system of agriculturally based economic exchange rested in credit arrangements, reciprocal agreements, and trade networks that crossed social classes and regions within the South, as well as taking in Caribbean planters, with whom well-off planters often had close relationships.

The plantation became the distinctive southern rural institution. The romantic myth of the noble southern planter, of aristocratic lineage, and the southern lady—a chaste, saintly, and sacrificial figure—appealed to white southerners but also to northerners seeking imaginative escape from their more modernizing North. The reality was more complex down south. Before the Civil War, a planter was someone who possessed at least twenty slaves—a benchmark of power even more central than acres of land or size of crops raised. Planters were not common in the South, however. In 1850, only 384,000 southerners (of 8 million whites in fifteen slave states) owned any slaves. Still, planters dominated the life of the Old South because of their wealth.

Slave owners growing cotton were capitalists in their concern for the bottom line and through involvement in international markets for that crop. Large planters practiced a limited capitalism, however, because their labor supply was premodern, and they took part in local markets of barter as well. Recent scholarship sees plantations as exploitative and cruel work camps embedded in broad capitalist networks. Slaveless farmers were more removed from capitalistic imperatives, engaged in self-sufficient farming and livestock herding, thanks to the lack of fencing laws and to free-range grazing practices.

Slavery was the basis of a productive economic system, in which the South was enmeshed with northern merchants and traders and the whole financial world of England. But it was far more than a business. It became the basis for a particular outlook, with norms of behavior, expectations, and relationships defining planter family lives of privilege and shaping their cultures. It inculcated a temperament of mastery that affected everything from everyday life to politics. Abel P. Upshur, a judge of the General Court of Virginia, in 1839 called slavery "the great distinguishing characteristic of the southern states," and he insisted that it exerted "a powerful influence in moulding and modifying both their institutions and their manners." *Slave management* was the term that summarized ways to increase productivity, and planters employed such positive incentives as time off work, allowing the slaves to have personal gardens, and the giving of gifts. But negative incentives included flogging by masters and overseers; in a telling detail, South Carolina masters gave cowhide whips as gifts to other planters on special occasions. Planters broke up slave families, selling husbands away from wives and children from parents, to slave traders or other masters. The opening of new lands in the Old Southwest to American settlement in the early nineteenth century resulted in a mass migration of slave owners and their slaves to the area, each year bringing several thousand slaves, manacled and chained and marched from the seaboard South. The rape of slave women led to a visible population of mixed-race children.

The planter ideology, despite such realities, was a conservative vision of the good society, a patriarchy whose advocates used the metaphor of the family to describe the plantation world of the planter, his lady, children, and slaves. The plantation legend enshrined paternalism as the ideal and pictured the planter as a civilizing force in the South. The plain white farmers, the yeomen, supported a different version of agrarianism and one less romanticized than the planter legend. They were located not in the rich farmlands but in the isolated areas of the hill country, mountains, and piney woods. The yeoman ethic was an individualistic one of self-reliance, material acquisition, private property, and honorable behavior. Yeomen sometimes owned a few slaves and worked beside them in the fields, ate the same food, and lived in similar modest structures, but white racism bonded whites of all social classes.

The household was a structural foundation for daily life in the South, especially significant as the location of white women's cultural authority but also as a locus for the assertion of white male power. Most women had little opportunity for work outside the household; they defined themselves as mothers and wives. Plantation mistresses, and many yeomen women as well, made management decisions within the household, oversaw the development of children and slaves (including disciplining them), visited with neighbors and relatives, enjoyed music, read, kept diaries, and maintained a pronounced religious atmosphere in the home.

Slaves themselves were trapped in a system mostly beyond their immediate control. The term "slaves" is the historic one that suggests enslaved peoples were imprisoned in a system that tried to dehumanize them. The experiences of slaves from praying to singing to cooking to raising children showed the creativity they showed in coping with the system as best they could. They responded in many ways to it—some organizing small and large rebellions some simply not cooperating, others acquiescing to its realities, and still others escaping in dramatic individual stories or through the cooperative Underground Railroad. Religious faith gave a secure worldview above and beyond the power of any plantation owner, and folk customs and belief provided order and stability to slave society. Although states banned legal slave marriage, "jumping the broomstick" was a ritual recognition of marital bonds.

Republicanism provided the political philosophy at the heart of a southern worldview uniting a diverse group of people. It echoed the Revolutionary-era outlook that treasured the idea of independence above all else. Late eighteenth-century southern planters had embraced the country republicanism that came out of British political controversies and provided an ideology that saw power as evil and wealth as a corrupting influence. The increased capitalism that took root in the North led its advocates away from this country republicanism and toward modern liberalism, with a concern for free labor, central government sponsorship of internal improvements, a central bank that maximized nonproductive financial maneuvers, and growing power of the federal government to promote economic development. Antebellum southern agrarians, however, still saw land ownership and slaves as offering the best chance of remaining independent from corrupting influences and free of the debt to exploitive creditors that could restrain independence.

White southerners interpreted one key element of republican thought, Jefferson's ideals of liberty and equality, as representing a specific meaning of liberty—the slave owner's freedom to own slaves. With slaves in their midst, they had a tangible understanding of what the loss of independence would mean. An ethic of honor informed southern men's belief that their self-respect depended on how others treated them. Upper-class southern men resorted to the duel to defend their honor in such situations, while working-class men might launch into an ear-biting, knife-wielding brawl to preserve their public reputations for asserting their independence.

Politics and sectional conflict

Politics was the frontline of North–South sectional tensions and played a key role in nurturing a developing southern identity. The debate over the admission of Missouri to the Union in 1819–21 represented a new phase of southern political consciousness. The congressional vote on the Missouri Compromise in 1821 revealed the depth of sectional division at that point and reflected as well the injection of increased emotion into the interregional dialogue that dated back to the Constitutional Convention of 1787. The Missouri Compromise kept the regional balance in the number of free and slave states as new states were admitted to the Union. It drew a line, north of which Congress outlawed slavery. New conflicts arose a decade later with the nullification crisis that represented the beginning of the movement for southern nationalism. South Carolina challenged the power of the federal government to pass a protective tariff to encourage American manufacturing, because the state's political leaders believed a tariff would hurt southern agriculture. More broadly, the tariff touched deeper fears regarding the federal government's ability to legislate in ways affecting fundamental southern interests and restricting the freedoms of southern whites.

The Missouri debates and the nullification crisis furthered the development of a minority psychology in the South. The northern population was outgrowing that of the South, a situation that would lead to disruption of the free-state/slave-state balance in Congress. North–South tensions continued for three decades over control of the national government and the direction of national policy. The states' rights philosophy was a legalistic, literal-minded reading of the US Constitution as a way to protect the interests of southern slaveholders.

If politics saw the overt expression of regional consciousness after 1830, persistent racial fears propelled the gradual definition of the southern white identity in that period. Slaves represented about 40 percent of the southern population in the decades before the Civil War. Rumors of slave unrest appeared periodically, reinforcing white uneasiness. The Nat Turner Rebellion of 1831, a slave revolt led by a visionary slave preacher, resulted in the deaths of sixty whites in Southampton County, Virginia, and became a potent symbol thereafter for the potential of collective slave violence.

William Lloyd Garrison, one of the chief devil figures to southern whites, stirred southern white racial fears in 1832 when he began publishing the *Liberator*, a Boston antislavery newspaper that called for immediate, uncompensated emancipation of the slaves. He was one of the leaders of a strident new antislavery movement that stressed the immorality of slavery. Abolitionists portrayed the South as a corrupt society, whose white people abused their slaves physically, sexually, and morally. A prominent midwestern abolitionist, Theodore Dwight Weld, compiled *American Slavery as It Is* (1839), which recounted stories of slave-owner inhumanity. Weld's wife, Angelina Grimké Weld, and her sister Sarah Grimké, were from a prominent South Carolina family, and they were among several women abolitionists who were significant in injecting women's rights issues into the antislavery movement. Frederick Douglass was the leading African American abolitionist, using his experience growing up in slavery and his powerful rhetorical and writing skills to paint a grim picture of slavery and Christian slave owners.

White southerners developed a proslavery argument that portrayed the South as the best possible society, based on a stable and productive labor force and an orderly society. They used historical, scientific, and religious evidence to support their claims, as they contrasted the southern social system with the fractious labor scene in the free-labor North and its tumultuous, polyglot society. Modern capitalism there, according to the proslavery argument, was an exploitive labor system providing little protection for workers, whereas southern slavery was a paternalistic one that offered cradle-to-grave support for slaves from benevolent masters.

Religion, as well as political conflict and racial fears, played a crucial part in the growing regional consciousness in the South after 1830. Ministers gradually came to sacralize what one called as early as the 1820s "the Southern country" and its special needs, urging the establishment of new seminaries to educate young preachers in ways appropriate to the region. Protestant churches provided major institutional support for the development of a regional culture, beginning with the separation of southern Christians into three regionally organized churches: the Methodist Episcopal Church, South; the Southern Baptist Convention; and the Presbyterian Church, US. In each case, slavery was among the chief causes for separation. The idea of Americans as God's chosen people could be traced back to the New England Puritans, but by the time of the secession crisis, white southerners had invested piety into a South with a special providential mission, to extend slavery to new places.

The debate over slavery in the western territories, which the nation gained as a result of the Mexican War (1846–48), stirred political sectionalism to a new pitch in the late 1840s. Congress struggled between 1850 and 1860 to find ways to transcend northern desires that new western territories be "free soil" and exclude slaves and the southern insistence that slavery be allowed in the West. Inflamed passions and moral extremism fed violence related to sectionalism from the floors of Congress (a South Carolina congressman whipped a Massachusetts senator) to "bloody Kansas" (northern and southern sympathizers fought a war there trying to dominate the vote on whether the area should be slave or free land) to John Brown's raid in 1859 (an abolitionist attack in Virginia that sought to start a slave uprising). Each of these events added accumulating emotional and moral passion to the perception among people south of the Mason–Dixon line and the Ohio River that "a South" existed, with cultural, as well as political and economic, interests fundamentally different from those of the rest of the United States. Meanwhile, in the North, white southerners were perceived as a different people, a violent threat to the Union. The election of Abraham Lincoln in November 1860 became, for many white southerners, the final symbol of a northern conspiracy against their region.

Civil war

On December 20, 1860, South Carolina adopted an Ordinance of Secession declaring the state was leaving the federal Union. Six other states (Mississippi, Florida, Alabama, Georgia, Louisiana, and Texas) did the same in early 1861. The first battle of the war that followed was the Confederate attack on federal forces at Fort Sumter, South Carolina, in April 1861. After that, four other states (Virginia, Arkansas, North Carolina, and Tennessee) left the Union. All these states had considerable opposition within them to secession, and moderates generally controlled the state governments and the new government of the Confederate States of America, which a constitutional convention approved on March 11, 1861. The delegates claimed the legacy of the American Revolution, Americans fighting for self-determination against a distant, oppressive government. A portrait of George Washington—southern planter, American Revolutionary hero, and American president—appeared on the seal of the Confederacy. Mississippi's Jefferson Davis became the Confederate president. The southern section of the United States had now become a new nation.

The Confederate Constitution followed the US Constitution in many ways. It did, however, guarantee slavery in all territories of the new government and spoke of the "sovereign and independent states," rather than "we, the people." Notably, it appealed for the "favor and guidance of Almighty God." Confederate leaders admitted that slavery was the cause of the war; Confederate Vice President Alexander Stephens called the institution "the chief corner-stone of the Southern Republic" and state secession ordinances identified slavery as the concept that southern states were defending.

A discrepancy of resources became apparent as the war began. The Union had 22.7 million people, compared to 9 million in the Confederacy, a number that included 3.5 million slaves. The US government was an established national institution, with a navy and a regular army of 12,000; the nation's industrial capacity was converted to wartime needs, and an extensive rail network provided more transportation connections than did the far more undeveloped rail system in the South. The Union military strategy was to blockade the Confederate coast and invade the South from the Midwest and the North. In September 1862, a year into the war, Lincoln issued the Emancipation Proclamation, effective January 1863, making human liberty a goal of the war as well as preserving the Union.

Southerners did have certain advantages in the war effort. Many of the Confederacy's military leaders had trained at West Point and had experience in the Mexican War. The Tredegar Iron Works proved essential in producing innovative weapons, including torpedoes, submarines, and ironclads. Southern fighting men could see themselves fighting for basic human concerns in the face of invading armies—freedom, home, family, their land, and white racial solidarity. Their tribal religion told them they were fighting a holy war—the same language that northern ministers preached to their lay worshippers. Still, the South's infrastructure had been poorly developed before the war, and that reality presented many obstacles. Banks had inadequate financial reserves, inflation rose as the war went on, white southerners resisted heavy taxes to support the war, and food shortages appeared in cities and led to violent protests. When the government imposed conscription into the military, it became an urgent issue for many yeomen. Social class conflicts became strident, as the working classes came to believe they bore unfair burdens compared to planter elites.

The war undermined many features of southern consciousness, an effect that can be partially gauged through the experiences of women. Writers continued to praise the ideal of the southern lady, but women were left to run the plantations and raise the crops on small farms. They cared for the wounded under deplorable hospital conditions and found and shipped necessary supplies to men at the battlefront. The South's women experienced physical deprivation and the psychological trauma of the absence of loved ones and grief over the dead. They were spies in the Confederate service and, disguised as men, they served as soldiers as well.

War undermined southern ideology dramatically through the emancipation of slaves. Confederate culture championed the image of the "faithful servant," who stayed on the plantation and helped hide the planter family's silver from marauding Yankees or went off to battle with the young master. The Emancipation Proclamation was a symbolic landmark for African Americans— the Day of Jubilee. Congress approved the Thirteenth Amendment to the Constitution, outlawing slavery, in December 1865. The actions of the slaves themselves did more than anything to challenge ideology. Most slaves stayed on plantations during the Civil War, but many left as soon as Union armies approached. Slave plots and conspiracies in Virginia, Alabama, Mississippi, and Arkansas worked to undermine the institution of slavery. Thousands of African Americans fought for the Union to gain their freedom.

Although it was a momentous victory for human freedom, the Civil War undermined the southern economy in disastrous ways. The value of a $2 billion investment in land had diminished with the loss of the $3 to $4 billion in slave collateral that had financed antebellum plantation agriculture and whose loss promoted the creation of a new postbellum agricultural system using tenant farmers. A $3 million cotton crop was now in Union hands, factories were in disuse, banks lost financial resources and closed, public facilities had been damaged, and cities like Richmond and Atlanta lay in ruins. Damaged bridges, roads, and railroad tracks confirmed the image of a region in disaster; the absence of mules, horses, sheep, cattle, and hogs conveyed a disturbing visual loss for an agrarian society.

The human cost of the war was unfathomable at the time and ever since, as the South suffered 258,000 dead and 150,000 disabled. The war left orphaned children and created a generation of widows and maiden aunts. While the region's white people mourned their dead, they faced the central cultural question: Had the South they had constructed deep into the southern past died along with its political expression, the Confederate States of America? Some in the region even questioned God's ways, wondering how they could lose what ministers and other leaders had told them was a holy war.

Reconstruction

The Reconstruction era (1865–77) would be nearly equal to the Civil War in forging a self-conscious white southern identity. It set white southerners against northerners, on the one hand, and against southern black people, on the other hand. Reconstruction represented national efforts to incorporate the South back into the Union, with various national government plans designed to achieve this goal. In 1868 Congress passed laws imposing military rule in the former Confederate states, a system that white southerners called Radical Reconstruction. Constitutional issues of whether the South had legally left the Union at all occupied center stage in this period, and the Republican Party calculated what role disloyal white southerners should play in politics and government. Idealistic reformers, including religious men and women, came south to try to raise the region's people, whites and African Americans.

Reconstruction, in the end, left the South with positive achievements. Legislatures approved new state constitutions that would long continue as guiding documents for policy. Reforms appeared in judicial systems, in codes of government procedures, in the operation of county governments, in procedures for taxation, in methods of electing governmental officials, and in free public schools. Constitutional amendments provided crucial legal support in the twentieth century for the use of federal force to change the region's system of legal segregation.

Freed black people mostly stayed in the South after the war, seeking full incorporation into southern society. Although southern states enacted discriminatory laws regulating the work of African Americans in the years immediately after the war, freedmen and freedwomen nonetheless established a new society of key institutions that would provide the framework for their life in the emancipated South. Churches, schools, fraternal organizations, newspapers, social clubs, and businesses were only a few of the new activities that provided needed resources, knowledge, and opportunities to African Americans living in a world that seemed hopeful at the time for the future.

During Reconstruction, white southerners came to see white supremacy as the essence of southern society. Race had always been a central concern in the South, but when Radical Reconstruction granted political rights to freed people, it crystallized the evolving southern white belief that white supremacy was essential to the region's social system. Southern whites gave up slavery, but Reconstruction showed they would not surrender their deepest social commitment, which was to racial supremacy.

Ironically, despite racist beliefs by white southerners, much cultural interaction between black and white southerners had taken place under slavery. By the nature of the slave system, they were intertwined in ways that black southerners and white southerners would not be in later racially segregated worlds. Enslaved peoples lived and worked within white plantation and farm households, helped raise white children, and tended to the illnesses and deaths of white household members. Plantation mistresses had responsibility for the health of slaves on their plantations, sometimes tending them to recovery from illness. White male sexual exploitation of slave women resulted in a mulatto population whose origins were apparent. Black women cooked the food, under the supervision of the plantation mistress, that would come to define an aspect of a biracial southern culture. Evangelical religion gave a worldview, spiritual practices, and a music, among other features, that would cross racial lines, receiving different interpretations among the races but within a fundamental shared outlook.

Reconstruction became synonymous in southern white memory with the idea of outside intervention, of northerners trying to change the South. The term *Yankee* took on new degrees of menace beyond even those during the war. The South's history textbooks, popular novels like Thomas Dixon's *The Clansman* (1905), oral family lore passed down across generations, the film *Birth of a Nation* (1916), and the professional historical scholarship associated with Columbia University professor William A. Dunning all preserved the southern white memory of Reconstruction as an unprecedented time of corrupt government and outside meddling with the South's ways. African American scholars, including W. E. B. Du Bois, disputed such views, but white intellectuals and political leaders came to control the southern public memory.

Redemption is the term white southerners used to label their efforts in the late 1870s to end Reconstruction and regain control of southern governments. The term suggested the salvational meanings given to ending the most ambitious challenge to a white-dominated, hierarchical southern society. Radical Reconstruction was an experiment in biracial democracy, which led to numerous political and legal changes in the South. Whites used voter suppression, outright electoral fraud, and debilitating violence to keep African Americans from the voting booths or to ensure that officials would not count any votes they might be able to cast. The Ku Klux Klan emerged from the period as a recurring institution of white terror in the South and later in other parts of the United States.

Reformist northerners had worked since before the Civil War to reimagine southern society as more in tune with that in the rest of the nation through reforming southern ways. However, along with other people in the rest of the nation, they acquiesced to removal of federal troops by 1880 and acceptance of southern white control of African Americans in the South. White northerners and southerners reconciled at the expense of concern for black rights. The old abolitionist freedom fighter Frederick Douglass and other black leaders continued to campaign for racial justice as Reconstruction ended, but their voices were drowned out in the white-dominated public conversation.

Chapter 3
Tradition and modernization

After the Civil War, white southern ideologists minimized slavery's importance as a cause of the war. They romanticized the antebellum South into a myth of the Old South that refurbished the cavalier legend, whereby all southern white men were planters, the plantation mistresses were all ladies, and their slaves were contented indeed to toil for such fine people. Greater northern resources, in this mythology, had brought Confederate defeat, although its soldiers fought well, its leaders were better than northern commanders, and southerners had moral and religious characteristics far superior to northern fighting men. The religion of the Lost Cause invested enormous spiritual significance to a cause portrayed as a holy war against northern atheism. Elements that played a role in this story included the Confederate battle flag, the song "Dixie," the pervasive Confederate monuments, Confederate Memorial Day, the funeral celebrations of Confederate heroes, the rebel yell heard at sporting events and festivals, and historic sites identified with the Confederate cause. Veneration of the Confederate past was part of a broader embrace by white southerners of regional traditions.

One could argue that, even while it was backward looking in ideological content, the Lost Cause was modern at its birth. In the 1890s, promoters institutionalized the Lost Cause social movement in such centralized organizations as the United

Confederate Veterans, the United Daughters of the Confederacy, the Sons of Confederate Veterans, and the Children of the Confederacy. Fundraising drives financed the largest monuments put up in the South, the memorials to Confederate heroes, as well as supporting annual meetings, local social and cultural endeavors, educational activities, and veterans' assistance. The region's cities typically hosted annual meetings of these groups, making urban spaces—always centers of modernity—an anchor of the movement. This energetic social movement faded, however, after World War I, and the Lost Cause became less of a movement and more of a worldview that buttressed a white-dominated, backward-looking viewpoint. The Lost Cause movement had solidified in the last decade of the nineteenth century at the same time new laws excluded African Americans from any political role in the South and segregated them into inferior schools and other public places.

The New South that promoters of the region proclaimed in the 1880s and afterward seemed at the time the opposite of the Lost Cause, a progressive movement that looked to the future, calling for a diversification of the southern economy to encourage manufacturing and commerce. Journalists like Atlanta newspaper editor Henry Grady became prime boosters of this newly imagined South, with business owners emerging as new cultural heroes in the folklore of the region, portrayed as self-made figures, generated from the ashes of war. Such cities as Atlanta and Birmingham became the locales for New South dreams of economic development and progress.

The railroad was a transformative force in efforts to remake the South in the late nineteenth century. By the 1890s, railroad construction linked far-flung southern towns and crossroads with national and international markets and encouraged the spread of staple-crop agriculture beyond what it had been in the antebellum years. State governments provided funds to extend the tracks, corruption became rife as railroad companies bribed state officials

N144:-MOONLIGHT ON THE SUWANNEE RIVER IN DIXIELAND.

Away down upon the Suwannee River
Far, far, away,
There's where my heart is turning ever
There's where the old folks stay.

All up and down the whole creation,
Sadly I roam,
Still hoping for the old plantation,
And for the old folks at home.

46686

3. This postcard image of the Sewanee River evokes the dreamy romantic South that the myth of the Old South conveyed for generations after the Civil War, immortalized by poets in particular. The Spanish moss draping trees and the bright moon of the sky, shining on the river, were typical of the nostalgic imagery of the region.

for favors, and states gave away valuable land in hopes that railroad companies would come their way.

The textile mill became a symbol of the hoped-for New South, as New England mill owners came south as part of a southern crusade in the 1880s to attract industrial plants. Mill villages became the sites where countless rural southerners met the modern world. Using child labor, offering long workweeks, and paying low wages, the mills did, however, offer cash—and probably a better life than many had known as sharecroppers or struggling landowning small farmers. By 1915, the South produced more textiles than the rest of the country combined. Southern workers in factories and mines joined unions, but they did not become well rooted in the South. Manufacturers and commercial interests controlled great wealth and political influence that even translated into abuse of the criminal justice system to squash strikes and other unionizing efforts.

Chambers of commerce and rotary clubs attracted the ambitious, celebrating progress, a word that urban dwellers breathed in from the air, at least when it was not too polluted to breathe. New Orleans had long been the South's leading urban area, but in the twentieth century newer cities, notably Atlanta, Charlotte, Memphis, Nashville, Miami, Dallas, and Houston, became among the region's largest.

The countryside

Despite the growth of cities, the countryside remained the home to most people in the South until after World War II. The household was the focus of most peoples' lives, with family matters of central concern for black and white southerners, as people dined, prayed, entertained, sang inherited songs, gossiped about the community, and worked within the boundaries of extended kinship. The presence of black servants in households and on work crews highlighted the southern biracial context. Growing poverty for generations after the war meant a rural life marked by austerity. It was a violent world, from hunting in the woods, to fights on town streets, to public executions and spectacle lynchings of African Americans to assert white supremacy. High homicide rates reflected a culture of frequent social dysfunction, but also one in which the values of honor meant standing up for one's reputation, even if it meant possible death.

Religion was an anchor for rural southerners, who often were living through a vale of tears, with rugged living conditions, high death rates, and especially high infant mortality rates leading to much suffering; only religious faith could see meaning in it all. Membership in evangelical churches escalated after the Civil War, making the southern states those with the highest rates of church membership, attendance, and religious giving in the nation. White and black Christians worshipped in segregated congregations, yet worshippers shared a Protestant, mostly Baptist and Methodist, orientation. Protestant churches extended a pervasive moralism into southern life through campaigns for prohibition of alcohol, blue laws honoring the Sabbath, and restrictions on gambling and organized sporting activities.

If the term *New South* suggests change and even progress, one would have been hard pressed to see it in the agriculture that dominated the region's life. Farmers still concentrated on such traditional staple crops as cotton, tobacco, rice, and sugar, but the immediate post–Civil War adjustment to a new labor situation led to most freed slaves becoming sharecroppers. The crop-lien system provided the mechanism for financing the production of staple crops: sharecroppers worked the crop, but instead of paying rent on the land they worked, they would give the landowner part of the crop at the time of harvest. Sharecroppers often relied on the owner to advance funds for food, clothing, seed, agricultural implements, and even the mule to work the land. The system led to much sharecropper debt over the years, and it rested on the interconnections of race and social class exploitation. Landowners often preferred African American sharecroppers to whites because their racial status made it easier to take advantage of them. An Arkansas sharecropper in the 1930s explained how the system was weighted against him: "De landlord is landlord, de politician is landlord, de judge is landlord, de shurf [sheriff] is landlord, ever'body is landlord, en we ain't got nuthin'." The ever-present creditor–debtor situation, within unequal power relationships, made for interactions that were laden with racial hostility and abiding bitterness among croppers over several generations.

The idealized southern farm was far from sharecropping. In theory, it had always produced food crops and raised livestock to feed the family and then sold any surplus food crops. After the Civil War, more small farmers, black and white, entered the staple-crop market and diverted land for food to crops to sell for cash. When this happened in the 1870s and afterward, they ended up competing with new cotton fields in India and Egypt and faced global overproduction and declining cotton prices. Americans sometimes used the term *colonial South* to describe the southern economy within the nation and world. The region offered cheap labor to exploit natural resources and then served as a market for goods finished elsewhere. Poverty marked the South in the years from 1880 to World War II, making the region's people the poorest in the nation.

Southern farmers joined together, beginning in the 1870s, to address growing indebtedness, scarce credit, unfair railroad rates, fluctuating commodity prices, and other farm issues. An elite of well-off planters and commercial interests represented a southern establishment whose orthodoxy was small government, cheap labor, and low taxes. The agrarian reformers represented a social class rebellion against this orthodoxy, seeing answers to the farm crisis in the state and federal governments. In the 1880s, the Southern Alliance brought farmers together into a new organization known for developing cooperative programs aimed at economic reform to benefit farmers. It also supported Democratic Party candidates who would advocate such reform ideas as the subtreasury plan, whereby farmers could store perishable crops in local warehouses and receive loans on their produce while waiting for better prices. Women could join the alliances, supporting social and educational programs and serving as newspaper editors and lecturers, and evangelical ministers were prominent leaders of agrarian reform.

The Populist Party emerged in the early 1890s, winning significant state elections throughout the South but creating tensions with the Democratic Party, which had been the region's dominant party since Reconstruction. Populist leaders like Georgia's Tom Watson realized the necessity of appealing to black farmers for political success, at a time when African Americans could still vote in many southern states, and the party advocated political freedom and economic opportunity for all farmers. Although the party's leaders based their biracial appeal on expediency, they went far beyond

Democrats or Republicans in bringing white and black southerners together in a political movement aimed at achieving greater economic fairness in society. The 1896 national election proved disastrous for the Populists, muddied by a flawed alliance with the Democratic Party and suffering intimidation, voter fraud, and violence.

Assertion of white dominance

Although poverty might have created bonds across racial lines, poor whites focused their frustrations instead on keeping African Americans powerless, seeing them as competition for jobs and resources. To be sure, African Americans and white people in rural areas worked together, enjoyed the recreations of hunting and fishing, and visited the same country stores. Black women worked as domestics in white homes in towns, cleaning them, cooking the food white folks ate, and even nursing white children at times and helping raise them. Whites wanted social separation more than physical distance from blacks, making black subservience an everyday expectation. Jim Crow became the name for the southern system of racial segregation, named for a black-faced minstrel performer whose dance routine included the song, "Every Time I Turn around/I Jump Jim Crow." The song epitomized the performance of subservience at the heart of segregation.

In the 1890s, the folk customs of white dominance over black people—a shared attitude, North and South—became codified in law in all the former Confederate states and created separate, parallel black and white worlds. African Americans lived in separate parts of towns, kept run down by local governments to reinforce on black people their inferiority. Separate restaurants, schools, churches, water fountains, waiting rooms, and cemeteries were the norm for black and white southerners. Signs labeled "colored" and "white" visualized racial separation, and the soundscape was full of harsh and intimidating language for African Americans. An elaborate code of manners dictated

4. **Racial segregation created parallel (and unequal) worlds for white and black southerners. Russell Lee was one of many Farm Security Administration photographers who captured this image of an African American man at a water cooler between segregation signs outside restrooms in Oklahoma City.**

white–black interaction, although the specifics could vary from one place in the South to another. A servile manner shown by black people reflected white assumptions that they recognized their "place," but any assertiveness suggesting another key term in the southern racial system, "uppitiness," could lead to loss of jobs, beating, or even death.

Although white southerners came to believe this new legal segregation was ancient in southern society, it was not traditional, but rather a response to modernizing influences in the region. A black middle class emerged after emancipation, and white racial laws and expectations especially aimed at controlling the members of that class who might expect that education, a modicum of wealth, and professional status would limit racial degradation. The new postwar railway system created conditions that fostered confrontations between black and white people over race and class. When well-dressed African Americans bought a first-class train ticket and sat in the parlor car, whites often protested, believing the railroads should consign all black people to inferior smoking cars. The landmark Supreme Court decision in *Plessy v. Ferguson* (1896), which grew out of railroad seating issues, put the national legal stamp of approval on the segregation of public spaces in the South. It required that in states mandating separated cars, they must be equal for black and white riders.

Beginning in 1890, all the former Confederate states developed strategies to disenfranchise African Americans. They used poll taxes, advance registration far before elections, printed ballots to eliminate illiterates, residency requirements, and the "understanding clause" that required potential black voters to withstand the questioning of white registrars about their understanding of state constitutions. Violence and racial intimidation were also key factors in keeping black voters from the polls. The Democratic Party became identified with the "Solid South" in national elections. Rural politicians who appealed to racial fears emerged in the early twentieth century, tapping into poor white resentments at southern elites. Mississippi's James K. Vardaman, who served as governor and later as a US senator, dressed in a white linen suit, with white shoes, a broad-brimmed white hat, and a long flowing mane of silver hair—the visual embodiment of white supremacy. He spewed demeaning racial slurs and advocated lynching thousands of African Americans if necessary to ensure white dominance.

Lynchings in the South after 1890 became racialized, as groups of whites targeted African Americans considered threatening to the white supremacist society, especially those who challenged white economic power and did not work for white employers. Lynching generally meant hanging. The most common excuse for lynching was the claim of black men raping white women, but this charge was usually a cover for the raw exercise of white power to discipline the aspirations of black people, especially younger black men who had grown to maturity after emancipation. The most troubling expressions of the effort to impose white dominance were spectacle lynchings, whereby mobs of white people—including women and children—would gather in broad daylight for the slow torture of black victims. Large-scale race riots emerged as well in cities, including those in Wilmington, North Carolina (1898), and Atlanta (1907). Meanwhile, vicious brutality in the criminal justice system aimed at controlling African Americans through the convict-leasing program (where inmates worked for exploitative employers with little oversight) and later the harsh work routines of chain gangs and barbaric prison conditions.

African Americans and the Jim Crow South

The leading black spokesman was Booker T. Washington, whose book *Up from Slavery* (1901) charted his personal rise in society after the Civil War to become the founder in 1881 and long-time head of Tuskegee Normal and Industrial Institute. Located in the Black Belt of Alabama, that pioneering school promoted industrial education. Washington delivered perhaps the most notable speech in the late nineteenth-century South, speaking at the Cotton States Exposition in Atlanta in 1896. He proclaimed the Atlanta Compromise, whereby black southerners would defer political engagement and accept segregated society in exchange for white support for black economic and educational advancement. Washington took an accommodationist approach to white dominance in the South, but it represented a modernist outlook that worked within the limitations on black power at the turn of the twentieth century to inculcate middle-class ideals, a scientific approach to agriculture, and a probusiness ethic that fit the age.

Washington's approach faced increasing criticism, however, represented by the formation of the National Association for the Advancement of Colored People (1909) and the intellectual and educational work of W. E. B. Du Bois. Born in Massachusetts, Du Bois came south in 1885 to attend Fisk University in Nashville, taught in rural counties in the summers, and developed an enduring fascination with African American common folk. *The Souls of Black Folk* (1903) was a collection of evocative essays that included his insight on the "double consciousness" of the African American, a "twoness—an American, a Negro." He spent considerable time in the region, including teaching at Atlanta University and sponsoring annual studies of black social conditions (1897–1914). Du Bois insisted on the need to go beyond Washington's industrial education, advocating encouragement of the highest intellectual aspirations for African Americans and the training of a "talented tenth" of leaders.

Ida Wells-Barnett was a social activist who worked to counter lynching, as well as discriminatory aspects of southern law. Born a slave in Holly Springs, Mississippi, Wells attended Rust College there and taught in rural schools before moving with her family to Memphis, Tennessee, in 1884. She became a crusading journalist, and in 1885 one of her editorials denouncing a local lynching of three Memphis black men led to the destruction of her newspaper, *Free Speech*, and she fled the region. But she continued her crusade against lynching by means of widespread lectures in the North, a speaking tour of England in which she gained support of British aristocrats and social reformers, and a well-publicized meeting in 1898 with President William McKinley.

Migration out of the South became the most effective refutation of the social segregation and general powerlessness of African Americans in the region. "I'm tired of this Jim Crow," sang a bluesman, "gonna leave this Jim Crow town," saying he was "sweet Chicago bound." World War I opened job opportunities for African Americans in northern cities. Almost half a million African Americans in the South went north between 1916 and 1920. This demographic shift continued through the 1960s, with only 53 percent of black Americans living in the South in 1976, whereas 89 percent had been in the region in the 1910s.

The early twentieth century

Southern progressives were middle-class reformers who embraced modernity and accepted competition, expansive industry, and the market economy, but they wanted the economic system to embody more justice and efficiency. Specific southern problems associated with poverty, cultural backwardness, rural decline, educational inadequacy, violence, and poor health motivated many reformers to try to improve life for southerners. Women could not vote at the turn of the twentieth century, but they worked for uplift of those who were less fortunate and especially worked to improve children's lives. White and African American middle-class women helped to modernize public school curricula and resources, exerted pressure to regulate child labor in factories, and pushed for new forms of child welfare. Women gained new public roles through involvement in social clubs and church activities, culminating in the women's suffrage movement. Politicians in the region opposed giving women the vote, however. When Congress approved the Nineteenth Amendment to the Constitution authorizing women's suffrage in January 1919, 90 of 101 Democratic votes against the measure came from the South.

Politics in the Progressive Era revealed that reform came generally at the expense of African Americans. Progressive reformers embraced changes to make the political system more responsive. Direct election of senators, the private ballot (instead of voters publicly proclaiming which candidate they supported), and party primaries gave voters more direct control. In the South, however, political reform meant exclusion of African Americans from the franchise. A good example is the party primary, through which the Solid South Democratic Party asserted its primacy as, in effect, a whites-only party in the region. Winning the primary meant winning the election.

The era of Progressive reform came to a virtual end with the entrance of the United States into the Great War in 1917. The war became a modernizing force in the South. Prosperity came to the region, as the agricultural economy boomed and new industries appeared. The military located most of the training camps there, and the government built new munitions plants and shipyards along the coasts. White southerners fought and served overseas during the final 1918 campaigns in France, while African Americans served in construction and utility jobs and faced racist intimidation and violence in the South and elsewhere.

The pace of change quickened in the South in the 1920s. The textile industry thrived there, with almost three-quarters of textile workers residing in the region by the early 1930s. Tobacco factories spread after the war, especially in the Piedmont states from Virginia to Georgia, as the sale of machine-made cigarettes increased. The chemical industry had emerged during World War I, while the extraction of aluminum made Tennessee and North Carolina central places for that industry. Southwestern oil fields sprouted and brought increased wealth and more jobs. Tourism became a significant industry in the 1920s, especially with the development of Florida, whose climate attracted visitors, some of whom stayed and fueled the real estate industry in the state.

Rural isolation decreased thanks to Progressive-Era road-building programs, and rural people had new shopping alternatives through mail-order catalogs and chain stores that disrupted the postbellum country store monopolies. The automobile was a practical, everyday symbol of modernity. It increased mobility of southerners of all sorts and gave African Americans a consumer-stoked sense of status that was unusual in the Jim Crow world. The Ku Klux Klan grew in the 1920s, and its racism and violence fed images of the benighted South. The organization was as much a national one as a southern one in that decade, gaining political strength in areas of the Midwest and the Far West. The fundamentalist movement also reflected reaction against such modernizing intellectual trends as Darwinian evolution and "higher criticism" of the Bible by European theologians. The Scopes trial, in June 1925, dramatized issues of science versus religion but did not resolve them.

The Depression and the New Deal

The stock market crash in 1929 touched off an economic crisis that affected the entire nation. Annual per capita income in the South showed the Depression's traumatic mark on the region, as it fell from $372 in 1919 (already the lowest in the nation) to $203 in 1932. Starvation, homeless people, unemployed people digging through garbage dumps, suicides, declining health of people too poor to pay physicians—all showed the human toll of depression.

The Depression led to a drop in cotton prices to 4.6 cents per pound and a decline in the number of bales produced to 10,613,000 (from 14,096,000 in 1929). As economic hard times continued, many southern tenants lived in virtual peonage, with few alternatives. Industrial workers in the South as well as farmers suffered during the Depression. The economy of the region emphasized agriculture, so only 1.3 million people worked in industrial jobs in 1929, living with low wages, seventy-two-hour work weeks, and little power to affect their fate. Unionization efforts had failed, as manufacturers replaced recalcitrant workers with others needing work.

Traumatized people began to look to the federal government as the only possible solution to the Depression. The 1932 election was a momentous one, bringing Franklin D. Roosevelt into the presidency with the support of many southern Democrats. His New Deal agenda included programs for relief, recovery, and reform, few directly targeted at the South, but he came to see the region as what he called "the Nation's No. 1 economic problem." National programs benefitted the South disproportionately because of the need there. In 1933, Congress approved $300 million in funds for welfare, distributed through private agencies or state welfare departments, and the South received more than its fair share.

The New Deal addressed structural problems in southern agriculture through the Agricultural Adjustment Administration (1933), which paid landowners to take land out of production. It gave federal subsidies larger than the profits that planters would have received to harvest their crops and addressed a fundamental problem of overproduction in cotton and tobacco. The crop-limitation plans became the linchpin in the modernization of southern agriculture. These changes left tenants who worked the land without much redress and pushed sharecroppers and tenants off the land and into cities that were little prepared for their arrival.

The early New Deal's National Recovery Administration brought the federal government together with business to stimulate industrial recovery by establishing voluntary codes that industry leaders would support to maintain employment and stabilize wages and prices. The Federal Emergency Relief Administration sent funds for new welfare programs. The Public Works Administration (1933) and the Works Progress Administration (1935) employed people to work on permanent infrastructure projects. The federal government pushed along modernization in the South, helping to provide the infrastructure for the later development of the Sun Belt economic boom. The New Deal promoted cultural development in the South through projects in art, music, literature, photography, archaeology, history, and architecture.

The Tennessee Valley Authority became the most ambitious regional planning agency of the New Deal. It brought a better life to rural and small-town southerners through soil conservation, new roads, and more economic opportunities, even down to residential electricity and indoor plumbing, promoting

5. Ben Shahn was another Farm Security Administration photographer who captured the trauma of the Great Depression in the United States. He portrayed the world-weary despair of this tenant woman in Arkansas, typical of white farmers whose sharecropping indebtedness left them in poverty.

modernization in tangible ways. The centerpiece of the Tennessee Valley Authority was its dams, which generated inexpensive and reliable electricity, controlled flooding, enabled cheap electricity, eradicated malaria by destroying mosquito habitats, and contributed to soil conservation.

Franklin D. Roosevelt proved a charismatic figure for southern voters, who supported him through his four presidential elections. By 1936, Roosevelt had assembled an unlikely coalition—white southerners, ethnic Americans in northern cities, union members, and African Americans. The latter had long identified with the Republican Party as that of Lincoln and emancipation, but by the 1930s that party offered little to them. Migration north had created concentrated black communities, whose political influence became palpable in urban areas. The New Deal offered financial assistance to African Americans because of their poverty, even though it was not distributed fairly among the races in the South. Roosevelt became identified as an advocate for African Americans, with his wife Eleanor even more so, and southern whites ruthlessly vilified her.

Within the South, moderates and labor activists pushed the region leftward. The former achieved influence within federal government agencies and were active in reform groups such as the Commission on Interracial Cooperation, the Association of Southern Women for the Prevention of Lynching, and the Southern Conference for Human Welfare. More radical were labor organizers among coal and textile workers. From 1933, New Deal legislation promoted organization of unions, which encouraged textile workers to go on a massive general strike in 1934 involving 200,000 workers. Southern governors used their National Guard to put down the strike. The Congress of Industrial Organizations split off from the larger American Federation of Labor in 1937 and organized unskilled workers, launching organizing drives in such southern cities as Birmingham, Memphis, and Dallas. Violence and intimidation against union organizers discouraged workers from joining unions and made the labor organizer almost as suspect a figure as the civil rights activist to conservative whites.

Organized labor, big business, big agriculture, and big government were modernizing influences in a South that by 1940 had changed in many ways from the defeated region trying to rebuild in the post–Civil War era. But traditions held powerful sway to people who still lived mostly in rural areas and small towns more than in cities, did more farming than industrial work, and lived within a segregated racial system that still seemed rooted in slavery's legacy. On the eve of international conflict, the South remained a land riven by the juxtaposition of traditional and modern ways.

Chapter 4
Confronting change

The American South would be a major player in the national mobilization for World War II, which began with the Japanese attack on Pearl Harbor on December 7, 1941. Franklin D. Roosevelt hoped preparations for the conflict would promote economic development in a South still not recovered from the Depression. New military bases; aircraft, steel, and petrochemical factories; and shipyards along the coasts brought billions of dollars into the region—thanks to the federal government that southern politicians had often demonized. More than two million people from the South wore American military uniforms, many of them living outside the region for the first time. The war encouraged almost four million people to leave depressed rural areas for employment, two-thirds of them working outside the region. Personal income in the region more than doubled, and the number of industrial workers grew by 50 percent. The population of urban areas skyrocketed, cities suddenly full of country people come to town and roughly adapting to new ways, simultaneously straining urban infrastructures.

The exodus of southern farm workers for opportunities elsewhere led to labor shortages that upset southern landlords. This mood intensified in 1941 with the creation of the Fair Employment Practices Commission, an agency that, in principle, promoted equal treatment of African Americans and became a new target for states' rights advocates. Employers were so desperate for workers that African Americans were able to increase employment in defense industries as the war went on. Women also became prominent participants in the defense industries, from the heavy lifting in welding and riveting to clerical work to keep the vast military bureaucracy afloat.

Democracy became a watchword during World War II, as the nation fought against fascism and emphasized that democratic values had to be affirmed by all as the reason for fighting. The Double V campaign ("Victory at Home and Abroad") symbolized the need to achieve victories not only over fascism but also over Jim Crow. Black leaders stressed the necessity of racial equality, especially in employment, to gain that victory. Labor and civil rights organizations achieved victories in some southern cities in hiring and promoting black workers in industrial jobs. White workers often fought such gains, however, because they wanted to preserve their seniority privileges and white-dominated workplaces.

Economic development

The war, more than any single event, pushed the South far along the path of modernization. After its conclusion, military bases remained, as did industrial plants constructed for wartime needs, now transitioned to peacetime production to meet postwar consumer desires. The Cold War began shortly after the end of World War II, an ongoing diplomatic and military conflict between the United States and the Soviet Union pitting the ideals of freedom, democracy, and free enterprise against communism. Both sides maintained arsenals of nuclear weapons used as a deterrent to aggression and nurturing a military–industrial complex that had major impact on the South. Conflicts in Korea in the late 1940s and early 1950s and in Vietnam in the 1960s and early 1970s called southerners to war once more.

Southern prosperity came out of postwar economic investments by the federal government and private enterprise in the region's military establishments and research projects developing not just weaponry but also the latest high-technology projects. Defense industries became the largest employers in states such as Georgia (Lockheed) and Mississippi (Ingalls Shipyards). The National Aeronautics and Space Administration transformed Houston with its Johnson Space Center and made major economic impacts with the Marshall Space Flight Center in Huntsville, Alabama, and Cape Canaveral in Florida.

Mississippi's Balance Agriculture with Industry project in the 1930s had launched new southern economic development efforts, and other states followed. Planning agencies promoted the virtues of each state and assisted companies setting up plants, training workers, providing inexpensive or free land, and offering expansive tax relief for industrial recruitment. Real estate brokers, insurance agents, retailers, construction contractors, public utilities managers, bankers, media figures, attorneys, physicians, and other professionals became a new middle class that now guided civic life and influenced public policy.

By 1960, economic development had taken off to the point that per capita income had risen more rapidly in the South than anywhere in the nation. In 1940, southern incomes were 60 percent of the national average, but by 1960 they had risen to 76 percent. The South's economy by 1960 was more urbanized, industrialized, and commercialized than it was rural and agricultural. These changes would affect the context for the civil rights movement as well, so that by the late 1950s the southern middle class chose, in effect, to accept gradual racial changes rather than disrupt their economic growth and ties with the rest of the nation.

By 1960, half of southerners lived in cities, with less than a fifth still in rural areas. Television became a household necessity beginning in the early 1950s, with broadcast networks soon producing shows portraying either silly or virtuous southern characters and aimed at southern audiences. Air-conditioning became another household necessity, calming the effects of the heat and humidity that had defined the South for so long. That invention was revolutionary in the workplace, because the region now attracted northern businesses that had once avoided semitropical southern places, and in recreation, as movie theaters, restaurants, and sporting venues provided comfortable places to attract customers.

Racial politics

World War II had produced an assertive black leadership within the South, and the continued reform spirit of the New Deal led to aggressive campaigns for organized labor and for urban efforts to improve African American living conditions and opportunities. In 1946, the Congress of Industrial Organizations began its unionization effort, Operation Dixie, with great hope, but southern employers were as ruthless as ever in harassing and intimidating union organizers. They believed they had an advantage compared to northern industries in their maintenance of low wages and antiunion attitudes in recruiting new industries, and they refused to surrender it without a fight. The Taft–Hartley Act (1947) thwarted the Congress of Industrial Organizations and other union organizers with open-shop site requirements, allowing nonunion members to remain employed even if a union had been authorized.

The New Deal had identified economic issues as key to promoting improved race relations and the transformation of the South, but the immediate postwar years saw race emerging as the defining issue for many northerners thinking about the South. In 1946, President Harry S. Truman created the President's Committee on Civil Rights, and its report, *To Secure These Rights*, put the executive branch of the federal government behind a civil rights agenda. In February 1948, Truman sent proposals to Congress for a federal antilynching law, abolition of the poll tax, establishment of a permanent Fair Employment Practices Commission, and other measures that had long been liberal goals but now had strong presidential support. Later that year, the president issued an executive order desegregating federal agencies, including the military. However, southern political leaders were at the zenith of their power in the late 1940s and early 1950s, thanks to seniority and the power of incumbency in the South, and they blocked Truman's broader efforts.

The Democratic convention in 1948 was a startling event for white southern Democrats who could hardly recognize the new dynamics of the party. African Americans were a prominent part of the program, and the party platform endorsed civil rights goals. Disgruntled southern Democrats formed the Dixiecrat Party, seceding from the national party and attempting to take over the larger party's infrastructure in southern states. They assumed that the racial issue was paramount for southern voters, who would rally around the cause of white supremacy. The Dixiecrat convention in Birmingham rang with rebel yells, the singing of "Dixie," and displays of the Confederate flag—revealing the connection between the Lost Cause and white supremacist politics. The party nominated South Carolina's Strom Thurmond for president and Mississippi's Fielding Wright for vice president, indicating the Deep South's prominence in the party.

The Dixiecrats never became a popular movement, however, because it was the expression of an elite who thought they could appeal to white unity and use their understanding of the Democratic Party machinery to gain their goals. But they faced opposition from the urban press, moderate voices, and congressmen and senators reluctant to jeopardize their powerful influence over supporting this rebellion. Many businesses, as well as state governments, relied on federal government subsidies and did not want to endanger them. The Dixiecrats did gain more than a million votes in four southern states where they substituted their ticket for that of the national Democratic Party candidates.

Brown v. Board of Education

The Supreme Court rendered its decision in *Brown v. Board of Education of Topeka, Kansas*, on May 17, 1954, unanimously declaring that "separate educational facilities are inherently unequal" and nurturing a sense of inferiority among African American children. The National Association for the Advancement of Colored People's legal strategy of using the federal courts to promote racial desegregation gained validation with the decision, but it led in turn to southern state legislatures persecuting and, in some cases, virtually banishing the organization. The Congress of Racial Equality and the Urban League had also been working to bring change, gaining modest victories in northern cities and border states.

The *Brown* decision touched off a furious response from white segregationists. *Black Monday*, by Mississippi judge Thomas P. Brady, was the single most inflammatory and influential publication in its immediate aftermath, and he anticipated many of the arguments that segregationists would employ for a decade. He framed his protest in terms of defending the rights of those who "love our Constitution, our Government and our God-given American way of life." Brady sketched vile racist portrayals of African Americans little removed from the African jungle, now to be educated together with white children. White southerners who opposed school desegregation feared schools would become sites of interracial sex and marriage.

Some southern newspapers, in contrast, were moderate in their response to *Brown*. Some border South states and cities began complying with the decision, but most of the region's institutions waited. African Americans could see little progress toward educational desegregation in the immediate years after the *Brown* decision, because the Supreme Court did not push for immediate compliance with its ruling and President Dwight Eisenhower, no fan of the ruling, did little to enforce it.

The Cold War context of the court's decision was important in the South. The United States and its allies competed with the Soviet Union for the allegiance of the newly independent nations of the developing world, and the latter came to have serious doubt about whether the American racial story, exemplified by the legacy of southern relations and white resistance to social change, was a model to emulate. On the one hand, civil rights activists argued that changes in racial laws and customs were essential for the nation to defeat communism by showing that democracy could include people of color. American policy makers generally embraced this logic. On the other hand, white supremacists appealed to imagined links between the civil rights movement and communism to call for opposition to racial change to thwart communist influence.

Citizens' councils emerged as the leading white segregation pressure group. Their members were middle-class and upper-class white businessmen and planters. Founded in the Mississippi delta in July 1954, the council movement spread throughout the Deep South, where other similar groups formed. They became known as "respectable segregationists" and the "country-club Klan," but they could be ruthless in their intimidation and countenanced violence among some supporters.

The murder of Emmett Till in Money, Mississippi—not far from the birthplace of the councils—became an example of this climate and a pivotal moment in the emergence of a new activist stage of the civil rights movement. Till lived in Chicago but was in the Delta visiting family members in the summer of 1955, when a white woman, Carolyn Bryant, accused him of whistling or winking at her in a country store. The incident evoked the specter of the ultimate southern white taboo, interracial sex. Bryant's husband and other local men kidnapped and tortured the fourteen-year-old boy before dumping his body in the Tallahatchie River. Such murders had not been unusual in the South for generations, but the wide publicity around Till's murder exposed the violence and cruelty of southern society for the world to see. The murder was also significant as one of the first national and international media events in the age of expanding media reach, especially through television. Till's murder became the impetus for many African Americans in the South who soon became prominent members of the movement.

The term *massive resistance* dates from February 25, 1956, when US Senator Harry F. Byrd of Virginia proposed resisting school desegregation, and it came to include many forms of resistance from thousands of legislative enactments, speeches, writings, suppression of dissent, and, ultimately, the closing of public schools in several states. James Jackson Kilpatrick, editor of the *Richmond News Leader*, urged the southern states to interpose state authority over public schools between the local level and the federal government's decree. By mid-1957, eight states had such measures in place, and Virginia closed its public schools. North Carolina Senator Sam Ervin drafted an uncompromising statement endorsing interposition, and the overwhelming majority of southern senators and congressmen signed it in March 1956.

The desegregation of Central High School in Little Rock, Arkansas, in 1957 was the first showdown between the advocates of massive resistance and the federal government. The city school board authorized admittance of nine African American students, but white mobs prevented their enrollment through scenes of ugly violence. A reluctant President Dwight Eisenhower sent in the US Army to restore order, shocking segregationists across the region but making clear now that the national government would enforce school desegregation. The courtroom became the place where over the next few years federal judges overturned massive resistance

6. Six-year-old Ruby Bridges was the first African American child to attend an all-white public school in the South. Accompanied by her mother and US federal marshals, she was escorted from her school in New Orleans as a violent mob tried to intimidate her. She went on to become a civil rights activist and wrote of her achievement to inspire others.

strategies, whether plans to close public schools or to use public funds for private schools. The economic downturn in Little Rock after 1957 led moderates to cite the "lesson of Little Rock," as the economic cost of diehard resistance to change promoted compromise. Virginia moved away from interposition in the fall of 1958, as middle-class white moderates asserted their unwillingness to give up their public schools to maintain rigid segregation.

The civil rights movement

The Montgomery bus boycott (1955–56) had already begun a new phase in the direct protest against racial discrimination. Organized African American protests against segregation dated back to the nineteenth century, and the activities of union organizers, including the Congress of Industrial Organizations, in the 1930s and 1940s represented an even more assertive protest and led to the appearance of civil rights groups dedicated to reform. The Montgomery protest began when the seamstress Rosa Parks, an activist with the National Association for the Advancement of Colored People, refused to give up her seat on a bus to a white passenger, as the law required. The Reverend E. D. Nixon, a labor organizer, and the Women's Political Council, headed by Jo Ann Robinson, a professor of English, suggested a boycott of buses. The Women's Political Council formed in 1949, and in the mid-1950s it had several hundred middle-class black women as members who promoted such public policies as voter registration, hiring more black policemen, and desegregation of public drinking fountains. The boycott succeeded because of the widespread sharing of information about alternative travel possibilities for working black people, including many women who worked as domestics for white families. The Supreme Court invalidated the city's bus segregation, which ended in December 1956.

Dr. Martin Luther King Jr. emerged at the age of twenty-seven as the leader of the Montgomery bus boycott and symbolic leader of the black freedom struggle. Born to a black middle-class family with many preachers in his lineage, King brought the style and imagination of the southern black church to his role as civil rights leader. The social gospel of American Protestantism, which taught the need to use Christian conversion as an impetus to achieve the kingdom of God on earth, shaped his development of a philosophy of social protest. The Personalist philosophy taught him that segregation scarred the soul and degraded the individual human personality that was part of a broader divine, universal personality. Nonviolent philosophy became another key feature of his thinking and leadership of the civil rights movement. Black religious tradition emphasized the dignity and worth of all people, and God was a personal and loving God who intervened in the life of His children. King synthesized these influences into the idea of the Beloved Community—the hope that the end of segregation would be followed by a color-blind inclusiveness based on love and justice to foster true brotherhood. King aimed to empower people so long demeaned and disrespected, and he initially had confidence that southern white Christians would respond to peaceful protest. His repeated experiences of the moral failures of white Christians to support the civil rights cause led to his deep frustration and disillusionment, reflected in his *Letter from Birmingham Jail*, addressed to white moderate preachers.

King and his associates launched a new organization, the Southern Christian Leadership Conference (SCLC), in 1958 to spearhead community-based direct-action projects in Albany, Georgia; Birmingham, Alabama; St. Augustine, Florida; and Selma, Alabama. The SCLC drew from local leadership and community organizations that revealed the civil rights movement was one led by local people as much as region-wide activists. Baptist minister Fred Shuttlesworth in Birmingham, for example, was a fiery and fearless fundamentalist preacher who had long been involved in efforts to reform that city, a figure whom SCLC relied on to push Birmingham's brutal racial regime into change. Fannie Lou Hamer was a poor sharecropper, as powerless as any black American in postwar America, but she responded to calls for voter registration in the early 1960s. She became a down-to-earth, grassroots activist who gave legitimacy to outside organizers coming into the Mississippi delta by embracing their work to sharecroppers often skeptical of outsiders. The assassination of the National Association for the Advancement of Colored People's leader Medgar Evers in 1962 symbolized the risk of protest, as did the murders of three civil rights workers in Mississippi in 1964. The civil rights movement by the early 1960s drew on widespread popular support among African Americans. Many of the movement's leaders were church men and women, anchoring the movement in the enduring African American religiosity that had been forged since slavery.

The sit-ins began in February 1960 when four students at North Carolina Agricultural and Technical College in Greensboro sat at a lunch counter attempting to desegregate it over food. Student sit-ins spread across the South, with 50,000 or so people taking part in some 100 cities. They reflected a generational shift in protest to the young, who were showing impatience with the lack of progress. These protests shattered the fragile racial peace of the South, as city administrators and business leaders had adopted a temporizing strategy that hoped to maintain civility in negotiating with community groups pressing for change.

The sit-ins gave birth to the Student Nonviolent Coordinating Committee (SNCC), with such prominent civil rights activists as James Lawson, John Lewis, Marion Barry, James Bevel, and Diane Nash becoming leaders in the new group. It brought innovative tactics, increasing militancy, a heightened sense of racial consciousness, and an emphasis on decentralized organization and work in local communities. Members of the SNCC became key participants in the Freedom Rides of 1961 sponsored by the Congress of Racial Equality, which tested the constitutionality of segregated seating on interstate buses. That same year, Robert Moses launched a voter registration project. In 1964, the Mississippi Summer Project enlisted large numbers of white college student volunteers as fieldworkers, leading to the formation of the Mississippi Freedom Democratic Party. "Freedom schools" educated some 2,000 students at forty-one schools in the state.

The battle of Birmingham was a dramatic and bloody event that nonetheless marked the movement's progress. In 1962, Alabama elected as governor George Wallace, a fiery populist committed to opposing integration. Wallace defied a court order in resisting integration of the University of Alabama and worked with political allies in Birmingham to frustrate the SCLC campaign that began in April 1963. The city had a long history of violent resistance to civil rights efforts, earning it the name of "Bombingham." Its political disorganization and lack of civic leadership on civil rights

7. Ku Klux Klan members marched in a parade in Montgomery, Alabama, in December 1967, carrying American and Confederate flags. The Klan reappeared in the 1950s in response to the civil rights movement and often displayed the Confederate battle flag as a symbol of white supremacy.

left default control to Eugene "Bull" Connor, the pugnacious police commissioner. The SCLC took a risk and recruited elementary and high school students to take part in the demonstrations. They were met by fire hoses and police dogs that created chaotic and violent scenes that network television broadcast nationwide and newspapers headlined around the world. The city reached an agreement that gave the SCLC enough concessions to mark a victory. The violence continued as segregationists killed four young girls attending Sunday school during a bombing at the Sixteenth Street Baptist Church in September 1963.

Leaders of the civil rights movement had, nonetheless, regained momentum after Birmingham, reinforced by a new commitment by President John F. Kennedy to support national civil rights legislation. In June 1963, Kennedy addressed the nation, insisting that "we are confronted with a moral issue . . . as old as the

Scriptures and as clear as the American constitution." The emotional high point of the civil rights movement came in August 1963 when the various organizations of the movement sponsored a march on Washington to support that legislation. King delivered his inspirational "I Have a Dream" speech, calling the nation back to the long-held American dream of freedom and opportunity.

The assassination of President Kennedy in November 1963 brought Vice President Lyndon B. Johnson to the presidency, and Johnson surprised many observers with his fervent championing of civil rights legislation. Johnson had grown up in poor rural country in central Texas and became a fervent New Deal congressman. He brought a tepid record on support of civil rights legislation to his presidency, but his conversion to the cause while president and his powerful legislative skills garnered bipartisan support for the Civil Rights Act of 1964. The law made discrimination in education, public accommodations, voting, employment, and housing illegal. Johnson pushed for legislation to assist those in need, including the War on Poverty, Head Start, federal school breakfast programs, Medicare, housing projects, and the Job Corps—representing together an ambitious and far-sighted Great Society that was worthy of its New Deal ancestry. Many of these programs had special impact in the South, beset still by disproportionate social problems and economic inequalities compared to the rest of the nation.

Protests in Selma, Alabama, in 1965 were the climax to the most dramatic stage of the civil rights movement. In January 1965, King announced a campaign for voter registration in Alabama. The local community in Selma represented the transformative power of grassroots protest, as hundreds of black teachers, funeral directors, and barbers marched for the vote. On March 15, President Johnson addressed a joint session of Congress and endorsed a strong voting rights bill. King led a Selma-to-Montgomery march that spring, resulting in Alabama state troopers savagely beating marchers on the Edmund Pettus Bridge in what became known as Bloody Sunday. Johnson activated the National Guard, and on March 21, 2,000 federal troops accompanied marchers from Selma to Montgomery. White onlookers shouted insults and waved Confederate flags, evoking once more the Lost Cause in defiance of impending social change. But change was palpable. The Civil Rights Act of 1964 and the Voting Rights Act of 1965 overturned state segregation laws and disfranchisement methods, promoting the return of African Americans to southern politics. Black voting increased by 50 percent across the South within a few years. What had been the defining social and political system of the South for generations had been toppled.

The pace of change came at different rates across the South after the momentous legislation of the mid-1960s. Cities, national companies and franchises, federal offices, and the Upper South quickly adjusted to new expectations, whereas small towns, rural areas, mom-and-pop local businesses, and the Deep South lagged behind. Public accommodations were prime and public spots of change. The 1964 law prohibited discrimination at government locations and at any business engaged in interstate commerce, which covered many restaurants, cafeterias, movie theaters, sports arenas, and hotels and motels. Schools were another space where southerners adjusted to a new social system. In 1969, the Supreme Court's decision in *Alexander v. Holmes* mandated immediate and thorough school desegregation. Some white parents withdrew their children from public schools and propelled the growth of segregation academies. By early 1970, some 400 such schools enrolled 300,000 students. But by 1973, the South had the nation's highest rate of high school desegregation. Writer Willie Morris had graduated in the 1950s from Yazoo City High School, in the Mississippi delta, and he returned to the town in the early 1970s to chronicle the school's successful desegregation. He concluded that the restructuring of everyday life was "a true human revolution."

Many socioeconomic problems remained in the South after the civil rights movement, but its legacy of change was dramatic. The words on Fannie Lou Hamer's tombstone in Ruleville, Mississippi, captured the movement's human impact. The gravestone tells visitors that she and other activists worked to create a southern society where people "might be able to say they were no longer 'sick and tired of being sick and tired.'"

Chapter 5
The evolving South

The American South has always been a construct, an idea with various ideological, behavioral, and materialistic expressions. Observers have fastened many descriptors onto the region, including religiosity, violence, manners, hospitality, and provincialism, but few commentators familiar with the area by the 1970s would have denied that racial consciousness was a defining feature. African Americans had long exposed the racist structures of southern life, but in 1971, *Ebony*, the leading popular magazine of black life, published a special issue on the South. It praised its changes and pointed African Americans to look again at the homeland of so many people who left in the Great Migration. This publication was arguably the beginning of a southern turn in black American culture and coincided with the beginnings of a dramatic reverse migration as African Americans moved to the South. In September 1976, *Time* magazine published "The South Today" in the aftermath of Georgia Governor Jimmy Carter gaining the Democratic Party's presidential nomination that summer. It was a glowing report of the South's progress in race relations, economic development, and preservation of a distinctive culture with much to offer the nation. One essay, "The Good Life," focused on the South's spectacular beauty and extensive resources for recreation. But the good southern life was now one that embraced the integrated ideal.

Other observers, however, talked of the South that had disappeared by the 1970s, as technology, transportation, communications, mass culture, and the spread of federal government influence tied the nation together. But if this Americanization of the South occurred, so did the spread of southern ways to the rest of the nation. Country music radio emerged in New York City and stock car tracks appeared in New England, southern conservative politics became the Sun Belt conservatism that conquered the nation in the 1980s, the evangelicalism that had long dominated the South now became a formidable national political force, and the millions of black and white migrants out of the South in the twentieth century planted their cultures in nonsouthern places and shaped their future development.

Southern identities did not vanish, however; rather, they adapted to new contexts. As in the rest of the nation, people in the South moved to the suburbs after World War II, with backyard patios replacing front porches and deep-dug barbecue pits giving way to gas grills. Automobiles became ever more essential, as southern cities often rejected investments in public transit for more individualistic private transportation, creating clogged traffic and pollution. Suburban people reflected the new demographic development—the explosive growth of the middle class in the 1970s and afterward.

The experiences of women are particularly illustrative of these changes. Region-specific popular representations and cultural expectations have long been part of growing up female in the South. The images of white-gloved elite ladies or downhome Daisy Maes, the patriarchal demands of wife and mother, and the gender orthodoxies of fundamentalist religion still circulate in southern culture. The ghost of Scarlett O'Hara can be found in the contemporary South, but feminism, the sexual revolution, and the sometimes gender-related effects of federal legislation and court rulings have made for a very different context for women's lives.

Women embrace the role of wife and mother, but single mothers—the South has long had the highest divorce rates in the nation—and the need for affordable day care for children broaden family concerns in new ways. Women run small businesses, are professionals, and sit as mayors, governors, US senators and representatives, and judges. Federal legislation ensures concern for women's equality with men in employment, although they have not achieved equal wages. Working women became key figures in the southern economy, because the service economy that boomed in the 1980s and after relied disproportionately on women workers.

African Americans embraced the economic opportunities that appeared in the 1970s. Elected black politicians formed a new leadership group, working with black ministers, businesspeople, and successful professionals. Churches continued to be organizational sites for black political efforts and civic life, as were the social clubs that had long been a part of African American society. Martin Luther King Jr.'s ideal of the Beloved Community was an ongoing inspiration for racial reconciliation efforts that found black and white southerners working together to push forward social justice.

As time went on, the South increasingly appeared as "home" in sometimes nostalgic black memoirs and other literary imaginings. They juxtaposed such positive views with unflinching recollections of Jim Crow discrimination. The rural South embodied primal connections to the African homeland. Alex Haley's novel *Roots* (1976) raised up African civilization as a noble one and launched a new interest in genealogy among black Americans in general. Black culture embraced such rural southern tropes as home, community, family, food, and church. Black creative people from Alvin Ailey's "Revelations" dance series, which celebrated his rural Texas youth, to the films of Tyler Perry set in the rural South, to the "Dirty South" music of rappers like OutKast all pointed audiences to the South as a creative place for African Americans.

8. Before the invention of air-conditioning, cardboard fans, attached to wooden sticks, were pervasive in southern churches to keep the air moving during the often-lengthy services. Funeral homes, insurance companies, and other businesses would buy the fans in bulk and distribute them free to churches. This fan, from the Standard Burial Association in Natchez, Mississippi, in the 1960s, boils down the spiritual message to its essence.

The 2000 Census reported that the black population of the South grew in the 1990s by 3.5 million, some 58 percent of the increase in the nation's African American population. Much of the increase resulted from a return migration of black people to the South, a population shift that began in the 1970s, when 1.9 million black people came to the region, and continued in the 1980s with 1.7 million black returnees.

A complex economy

Economic development drove the rising middle class, as southern states continued the diversification of their economies. States and local communities had economic development agencies or commissions, and even small towns boasted of industrial parks. The *Sun Belt* became the term for a now-prosperous, fast-growing, and urbanizing South, attracting northern and international investment and gaining a large percentage of federal funding through government programs. The media played a key role in presenting attractive images of this modernized place.

Agribusiness replaced family-run farms, with computers operating cotton gins and seasonal Latino workers picking Florida oranges and Mississippi delta soybeans. Diversification of crops was now the norm, as south Georgia peanuts and Delta catfish became profitable. Woodland and pastureland that had once produced cotton now supported the region's livestock industry, as cattle, hogs, and poultry became ever more economically significant. Vertical integration for the mass marketing of beef, pork, and chicken promoted centralized corporate control of the entire production process. The service economy loomed large in the South; Arkansan Sam Walton's Walmart became a behemoth big-box store that provided inexpensive merchandise and numerous, if often ill-paid, jobs for the working classes.

Tourism was another economic dynamo, seen in the neon-lit casinos of Tunica, Mississippi, in Gulf Coast condos, in the revitalized downtown district of Beale Street in Memphis and the riverfront in Chattanooga, and in the historic districts of Charleston and Savannah. Dollywood and Graceland were among the most popular tourist attractions in the South, drawing people attracted to two of the region's acclaimed musical talents, Dolly Parton and Elvis Presley. Disney World drew families from around the world and made Orlando a fantastic landscape of bungee-jumping enthusiasts and recreated Taj Mahal landmarks—and one of the region's largest cities.

An economic downtown downturn occurred in other places, however, as deindustrialization shook the southern textile, apparel, and furniture industries beginning in the 1990s. Workers in the Carolina Piedmont had worked for low wages, but they could not compete in the global economy with workers in Bangladesh and Mexico City. The North American Free Trade Agreement in 1994 resulted in several southern states losing a quarter to a third of their manufacturing jobs in the next decade.

Some people did very well indeed in the new global economy, but many others did not. The Bible says that the poor ye shall have with you always, but some conservative lawmakers seemed to have misinterpreted the saying as being one of the commandments. The endemic and far-reaching poverty of the earlier sharecropping economy had been broken, but most of the nation's rural poor were southerners, and urban poverty could be as bad in the region as anywhere. These people were often the working poor, toiling longer hours than their big-city counterparts, and were just as bound by the limitations of being part of an underclass. The white working class and lower middle class held their grievances hard, as they competed with African Americans after the 1960s for jobs and government resources. Racial integration affected these classes more than elites: public schools and swimming pools brought white and black people together along social class lines, but many private schools and country clubs remained effectively segregated. The decline of organized labor contributed to keeping wage scales lower than in other parts of the nation and to lower wages.

A new political system

The Democratic Party had anchored the Solid South in national politics and was the only functioning party through most of the twentieth century, but "Democrats for Eisenhower" evoked the appeal of a conservative Republican and war hero to the changing South in the 1950s. Eisenhower's popularity represented a seismic shift in southern politics. Barry Goldwater voted against the Civil Rights Act of 1964 and established his credentials as an opponent of racial reform. He won four Deep South states in the 1964 presidential campaign, despite Lyndon B. Johnson's national landslide. Goldwater was a southwestern free-enterprise, states' rights conservative, presaging what would become the dominant white political sentiment in the region for several generations. Richard M. Nixon won the presidential election in 1968, as he appealed to white southerners he targeted in the aftermath of racial changes. The "southern strategy" described the Republican efforts to target southern white voters, a successful strategy that led to Nixon's landslide victory in 1972.

From the early 1970s on, two main political and social ideologies competed in the South. The first was an interracial reform perspective common among progressives with roots in liberal populism and the civil rights movement. An optimistic outlook that saw economic equality as a major goal of public policy, it welcomed the opportunity to deal with continuing African American economic, educational, and criminal justice concerns that had not been solved with the civil rights movement. It sought cross-racial political coalitions and proved their viability. Moderate and liberal white governors such as Reubin Askew in Florida, John West in South Carolina, Dale Bumpers in Arkansas, William Waller in Mississippi, and Jimmy Carter in Georgia brought African Americans into government and sponsored reform legislation to appeal to the working classes. The South soon had more black elected officials than any part of the nation.

The two Democratic presidents from the South in the period since 1970 represented aspects of the new Democratic Party and its ideology. Jimmy Carter, from the Black Belt of southwest Georgia, appealed to southern pride in his candidacy, making use of southern speech, Georgia music, and his Southern Baptist faith to connect with people in the region and reclaiming many white votes for the Democratic Party.

Bill Clinton, elected in 1992, grew up in Arkansas but was educated at Yale University and was a Rhodes Scholar at Oxford. Elected governor of Arkansas at age thirty-two in 1978, he identified as a moderate Democrat who supported balanced budgets and improved public services. Clinton ran as a dark-horse candidate for the Democratic nomination in 1992 and won a large electoral vote victory, despite winning only a third of the South's electoral votes. Clinton played on his southern identity both in the campaign and in his presidency, positioning himself as what one scholar called a "redneck hipster" who loved southern music and food and could communicate with the white working class and with African Americans.

Clinton represented a continuation of the progressive moderate, biracial ideology that had loomed large in the 1970s, but between Carter and Clinton, southern politics underwent a tumultuous change with the steady rise of the Republican Party in the region, led by Ronald Reagan and focused on conservatism—the second predominant ideology. Conservatism had deep roots in the South, going back to the antebellum defense of slavery and later strict constitutionalism and states' rights beliefs of leading southern thinkers and politicians. In the postsegregation reconfiguration of southern society, conservatives articulated a new outlook that rejected explicit racism but used code words to touch white fears of African Americans. Republican Party consultants and politicians in the early 1970s used color-blind language to oppose addressing ongoing issues related to race. They claimed the ideals of freedom of choice and freedom of association to oppose affirmative action programs and school busing. Suburban voters embraced an individualistic philosophy that disdained social concern in favor of low taxation and business-dominated public policies. Elected president in 1980, Reagan was a Californian with few connections in the South itself, but he became the quintessential political expression of the Sun Belt ties between the South and Southwest. Positioning himself as a friend of white southerners, he touched on white racial anxieties.

Religion proved a key factor in the new southern political conservatism that percolated in the 1970s, gained power with Reagan's presidency, and has flourished ever since. The new religious right grew in response to social changes of the 1960s and took its place as part of the broader conservative movement. The Moral Majority, a lobbying and educational organization that supported conservative Christian causes, formed in 1979, the year before Reagan's election. Such later groups as the Religious Roundtable and the Christian Coalition formed key constituencies for the new Republican Party that triumphed in the South. The religious right sought a moral agenda focused on such issues as abortion and homosexuality, which often concerned issues of gender and sexuality. The religious right has been a national movement, but many of its leaders, including Jerry Falwell, Pat Robertson, and Ralph Reed, came from the South.

The twenty-first century

People in the American South have long experienced the effects of globalization, but since 2000 the pace of international economic integration and transnational flows of goods and peoples have increased substantially. The growing power of transnational corporations shaped the restructuring of the global economy. In 2010, the southern economy represented the fourth largest in the world, with Charlotte the nation's second largest banking center and Atlanta another financial capital. Southern products and services went around the world, including Coca-Cola, cigarettes from southern tobacco farms, Delta airplanes, and evangelical Protestant missionaries. Memphis's Federal Express and Atlanta's CNN were regional giants that ranked among the world's most important communication forces. The South became the nation's new "automobile belt," thanks to factories established by such international car companies as Toyota, Nissan, BMW, Mercedes, Honda, and Hyundai in Tennessee, South Carolina, Alabama, and Mississippi. The region was both a force of First World economic power and a postcolonial society still living with the long aftereffects of plantation society's social relations, racial attitudes, and economic limitations.

The transnational movement of populations became a major part of globalization after 1990. In 2006, estimates indicated that more than 30 percent of all foreign-born people in the United States resided in the South. Most new ethnic southerners are from South and Central America, the Middle East, and Asia. Vietnamese came to the Gulf Coast South after the Vietnamese War ended, establishing fishing communities, while Laotians settled in the mountains of North Carolina. Some immigrants came with job skills, professional status, business experience, and academic credentials. Many immigrants from Southeast Asia have become owners of motels and convenience stores.

Latinos represent the largest immigrant population in the recent South. At first, a majority of newcomers were young, foreign-born men seeking job opportunities, mostly unskilled but contributing their hard work to the agricultural fields, construction and landscaping crews, and the messy work of poultry plants. As African Americans in the new southern economy moved on to work in the service sector, Latinos took jobs they previously had worked, driving the booming southern economy in the process.

The notable presence of diverse foreign cultures made for a new multicultural South in the twenty-first century. Immigrants contributed new cultural features to the specifically southern context, combining them with older ways. Spanish-language signs appeared in the southern landscape. Latino merchants operated *tiendas* that sold guavas and Mexican soccer team shirts. They introduced the patron saint of Mexico and the Americas, Our Lady of Guadalupe, to the South's iconography, her image found on candles and the back windows of an older southern icon, the pickup truck. Mexican restaurants became as common in southern cities and towns as traditional barbecue shacks.

Conservative southerners have pushed back against the multicultural changes, with resistance to new diversity and social change at the heart of political conflict since 2000. The old Solid Democratic South has been replaced by a new Republican dominance seen in state legislatures and presidential election votes. Nationally, the South is part of a "red state" belt, including rural, conservative areas of the Midwest and the Great Plains, places that seem left behind by globalization and out of touch with American cosmopolitan outlooks. George W. Bush won the 2000 presidential race thanks to southern votes, including a sweep of the eleven Confederate states. Bush put together overwhelming support of evangelical voters with suburban middle-class Republican voters. The increasing religious diversity of the South, represented by Latino religion, but also notable, in places, by the presence of Buddhists, Muslims, Hindus, and other faiths not previously seen in the South, created a new context for the evangelical Protestants who had once controlled the public life of the region. They are still dominant, but secularization and greater diversity in the region make them now only one of many political interest groups. Donald Trump won the 2016 presidential election by appealing to a conservative populism that had deep roots in the South, going back at least to George Wallace. The nonreligious, seemingly amoral big-city New Yorker nonetheless used his pugnacious style and clear-eyed total support of evangelical concerns, resentment of Democrats, and economic appeals to gain even greater support among evangelicals than Bush had won.

The multicultural South has nonetheless had its political successes. The election of Barack Obama as president in 2008 and his reelection in 2012 suggested the eroding of the Solid Republican South in presidential elections, as he won Virginia, North Carolina, and Florida. Obama had no direct ties to the South, but he embraced the legacy of the civil rights movement and put together a coalition of people of color, women, and young voters that achieved his election.

The political and cultural divisions of the South have material expressions in the commemoration of two historical events that have defined the South—the Civil War and the civil rights movement. The Lost Cause ennobling of the Confederate memory dates to the late nineteenth-century efforts to celebrate the cause as an honorable and a sacred one based in states' rights constitutionalism, with slavery a minor issue. Defenders of the Confederate battle flag and the playing of "Dixie" believe they honor the region's past and its ancestors, including family members. The flag flew over troops fighting for slavery, however, and the Ku Klux Klan raised it in opposition to the civil rights movement—associations that critics cannot ignore. One rarely sees the Confederate flag on public display in recent times, even though it was once pervasive. "Dixie," similarly, is seldom heard except at Ku Klux Klan rallies.

Although the arc of change is apparent, the battles to remove these emblems were hard-fought. In June 2015, a young white supremacist, Dylann Roof, entered the Emanuel African Methodist Episcopal Church in Charleston and killed nine church members. Online images of Roof displaying the flag brought outrage, and Republican Governor Nikki Haley led the effort to remove the flag from the South Carolina capitol grounds. Alabama Governor Robert Bentley had the authority to take down the flag from the Alabama capitol and did so the same year, partly as a result of what happened in Charleston. Confronting the Confederate public heritage since then has focused on Confederate monuments. New Orleans took down the Robert E. Lee monument from Lee Circle as well as other memorials to the Confederacy in May 2017. The city government in Memphis, Tennessee, tried for several years to remove the city's equestrian statue of Nathan Bedford Forrest, a Confederate general, slave trader, and founder of the Ku Klux Klan, but faced delays from the Tennessee state historical commission. In 2017, the government sold the statue and the park it was in to a nonprofit, which removed the statue.

While these developments affected the commemoration of the Confederacy, southerners have deepened their collective memories of the civil rights movement. Maya Lin's memorial to those victims killed in the movement is at the Southern Poverty Law Center in Montgomery; Jackson, Mississippi, has a monument to Medgar Evers; the University of Mississippi honors its first black student, James Meredith, with a statue on campus; and Arthur Ashe now stands in statue on Richmond's Monument Boulevard, near the images of Robert E. Lee, Stonewall Jackson, and Jefferson Davis. Civil rights museums in Memphis and Birmingham have long attracted visitors. The state of Mississippi opened its civil rights museum and museum of state history, at the cost of $90 million in state-appropriated funds and another $20 million in private donations, in December 2017, justified in terms of their educational potential, their role in racial reconciliation within the state with the most fraught racial history, and their potential contribution to tourism. Civil rights trails in Alabama and Mississippi were efforts to promote cultural tourism among African Americans and others. History thus remains central to southern identity, but the version seen in public venues now is very different from that seen through most of the region's past.

Chapter 6
Creative words

Writing in 1917, Baltimore editor H. L. Mencken skewered the American South as "the Sahara of the Bozart," a place barren of culture and backward in attitudes, blaming this sad state of affairs on the rural nature of life in the region, a religious orthodoxy that stifled creativity, and general decline since the Civil War. Pervading poverty, high illiteracy rates, and lack of cultural infrastructure to support such institutions as symphonies, ballets, libraries, and first-rate universities and schools meant that in the early twentieth century the region did indeed inadequately support certain kinds of creative and intellectual life. But soon after Mencken wrote his critique, the region became the home to a vital cultural explosion, seen in such modernist writers as William Faulkner, Richard Wright, Thomas Wolfe, Eudora Welty, Katherine Anne Porter, and Carson McCullers, who appeared after 1930. Their themes of agrarian life, the memory of the Old South and the Civil War, religious values, the tensions of the biracial society, and the modernization of society connected their literary achievements with southern life itself.

An agrarian culture took root early in southern history, providing a foundation for cross-South cohesiveness, spreading westward through the nineteenth century and surviving the Civil War. Rural and small-town people dealt with each other in a face-to-face society, gathering around courthouse squares and country stores and discussing crop cycles, community gossip, and political scandals. A foundational religious worldview based on a widely shared evangelical ethos gave meaning to sometimes mysterious happenings. It was a deferential society, with a hierarchical class system based in differences in wealth, gender, and skin color. Orthodoxy could stifle free thought, yet it allowed for private eccentricity as long as the untouchable racial and patriarchal foundations of the society did not seem threatened. Conflicts could be rife beneath the veneer of community harmony, tensions among family and denominational members could erupt and tear apart institutions, and conflicts could easily lead to violence despite a mannerly way up to that breaking point. The region's two predominant ethnic groups, white people from western Europe and black people from West Africa, contributed folk aesthetic principles of symmetry and balance in the first case, and improvisation in the second, that combined in the particular natural environment of the rural South to produce a new material and spiritual culture as background for the writers, musicians, cooks, chefs, and other creative types who appeared.

In writings on the South, the land has always loomed large, as it offered the central context for southern life in the folk society that long dominated the region. Although the South was not unique in generating attachment to a place, southern writers and others have long seen that quality as an identifiable one in understanding the region as a particular construct. The contemporary African American novelist Jesmyn Ward is from Mississippi, and she notes that for writers, place infuses character, showing how "they understand the stories of their lives." She identifies with the "legacy of great Mississippi writers . . . all of whom were marked by living here." In origin, the sense of place associated with the South came from white conservative modernist figures, but Ward and other writers use place now to illuminate the harsh lives of their poor African American characters.

The environment has offered southern artists a place that stimulated their senses, and they used the sensory South, the extravagant vegetation and wildlife; the turbulent thunderstorms, hurricanes, and floods; and above all the stifling heat and humidity of the climate to signal that one was in an identifiable locale. The attachment to a place identified by observers as southern also grew out of the cultural memory. Writers could look around and see customs, rituals, and ways that connected to generations of people who had experienced farm-centered and small-town lives. History has always loomed large in the region. The legacy of slavery and defeat in the Civil War has continued to shape the social and economic life of the South. This sense of place could be a sentimental and nostalgic memory, but often it was one that recalled fragmented, frustrated lives, bereft of opportunities for people to do more than survive.

Few features of southern life were more important to the context of creative expression than the folk culture's orientation toward the oral and its encouragement toward a facility with language that emerged from a society appreciative of conversation and storytelling. William Faulkner noted of southerners, "We need to talk, to tell, since oratory is our heritage." Narratives of southern life might be folk tales, biblical accounts, family legends, or community memories. Eudora Welty remembered going for a Sunday ride with her mother and her mother's friend, sitting between them and telling them to talk. She saw such an experience as typical for southern writers who converted stories they heard into written works. Bluesman Son House saw a similar dynamic in song: "They'd sing about their girl friend or about almost anything—mule—anything. They'd make a song of it just to be hollering." Blues singers often came from churchgoing families, and the songs, stories, proverbs, and sermons they heard in spiritual spaces were also part of a culture whose sacred and secular dimensions rubbed up against each other. Folklorist and novelist Zora Neale Hurston identified a specifically southern, biracial facility with language, observing that "an average

9. Eudora Welty was an iconic Mississippi writer who won the Pulitzer Prize for her novel *The Optimist's Daughter* (1968). Her short stories and novels of southern family and community life beautifully captured the voices of a wide range of men and women, black people and white folks, rich and poor.

Southern child, white or black, is raised on simile and invective," taking their comparisons out of barnyards and woods.

Although southern whites maintained a rigid racial identity and could enforce it ruthlessly, from early on black people and white people heard each other's stories and songs, which became a foundation of the cross-racial interaction that informed southern culture. Many ethnic groups contributed to the southern mix, but the biracial context is especially significant. Living on southern soil for centuries, Euro-Americans and African Americans developed two societies, two cultures, but they also exchanged cultural knowledge. Sights and sounds of southern life revealed these interactions. They could be the intimacy of interracial sexual encounters that produced people labeled *mulattoes*, the community exchanges of musical forms, black and white women cooking foods in kitchens and combining African and European ingredients and cooking techniques, or the violent racial traumas that could erupt like southern thunderstorms.

Mencken saw the South as the "Bible Belt" (a term he invented), a place where one could not expect culture to flower. The South was, he said, "a cesspool of Baptists" and "a miasma of Methodists." Religion has, however, been a major factor in the cultural expressiveness that came from many southern places and genres, as creative people took seriously the images, symbols, and worldviews of the evangelical Protestantism that has long dominated the region. William Faulkner pointed to his childhood in a small town in Mississippi, where he grew up with religion all around him: "I assimilated that, took that in without even knowing it. It's just there." As a result of religion's looming presence, Faulkner, like other southern writers, used biblical stories, characters, and themes in his work.

The land, folk culture, sense of place, storytelling and language, interracialism, and religion were all factors, then, in nurturing creativity in the South, nowhere seen better than in southern literature. It has long been an analytical category for scholars, a marketing category for book publishers and bookstores, and a familiar concept for readers around the world. Writers went from being outliers in the national culture in the early nineteenth century to acclaimed in the twentieth. In the middle decades of the twentieth century, writers from one southern state alone, Mississippi, won one Nobel Prize; eight Pulitzer Prizes for fiction, drama, and journalism; and four New York Drama Critics Circle awards.

The nineteenth century

Early nineteenth-century writers generally became defenders of slavery against abolitionist attacks. They portrayed the plantation as an idealized place of harmonious social relations. John Pendleton Kennedy's *Swallow Barn* (1832), set in a decaying but genteel James River plantation in Virginia, established the romantic genre of plantation fiction, with its pastoral images, that would not only flower before the Civil War, but also be renewed after the war through the writings of the Virginian Thomas Nelson Page. His stories evoked a moonlight-and-magnolias world resting in nostalgia, using old slave characters reminiscing on the "good old days" and creating the myth of the Old South. The myth claimed an aristocratic, chivalrous plantation as the distinguishing feature of southern life. Harriet Beecher Stowe's *Uncle Tom's Cabin* (1852) had drawn on the conventions of plantation fiction, but undercut their romanticism of southern life in the politically influential novel that Abraham Lincoln once claimed had helped bring on the Civil War through its sentimental portrayal of victimized enslaved people.

Slave narratives became a key African American literary form, initiating a long tradition of protest that has characterized black writing and presented a very different picture of southern life than plantation fiction. Slave narratives portrayed cruel masters and mistresses and slave traders breaking up black families, undercutting any romanticized images of happy and submissive slaves. Frederick Douglass's narrative, which first appeared in 1845, showed him burning for freedom but constrained by harsh slave owners. Harriet Jacobs's *Incidents in the Life of a Slave Girl* (1861) portrayed a virtuous young slave woman maneuvering through a social system that encouraged sexual exploitation.

If slave narratives debunked the idealized plantation myth, the southwestern humorists of the 1840s and 1850s presented another, more gritty version of southern life than the mythic plantation. They were physicians, attorneys, editors, and politicians who wrote newspaper stories about life they had seen in the Deep South, known then as the Old Southwest. Authors wrote these tales in a vernacular tongue common in everyday life at the time, frontier sketches and fictional pieces portraying realistic, bawdy, rowdy, often violent people. Cotton plantations boomed in the newly planted rich soils of the Black Belt—that area of Georgia, Alabama, and Mississippi opened up for expanded settlement with Indian removal. Settlers made money quickly and lost it in the same rush through gambling and bad investments. Sut Lovingood, the creation of George Washington Harris, was a typical rip-roaring comic figure who spoke in regional dialect and behaved with wild abandon fitting to his time and place. Another such character, Simon Suggs, caught the spirit of the times when he said, "It is good to be shifty in a new country."

A local color genre emerged in the 1880s with picaresque stories of peculiar people in often-isolated and rural areas of the South. Authors penned stories for well-paying northeastern magazines and book publishers providing entertainment for the expanding middle classes who seemed interested in the most outlandish and oddest characters and places. One of the earliest was George Washington Cable, who wrote of the Creole families whose origins blended French and Anglo heritage in south Louisiana. They were exotic to readers outside the area, but he saw deeper social significance in the decline of aristocratic families and their racial arrogance that he came to see applicable to the South as a whole. John Fox Jr. was a Kentuckian who wrote of the mountainous region along the Kentucky–Tennessee border, romanticizing the traditional culture there. *The Trail of the Lonesome Pine* (1908) was a novel that helped to create the image of Appalachia as a distinctive part of the South.

Georgia's Joel Chandler Harris wrote of plantation life before the war, but he went well beyond the moonlight-and-magnolias plantation genre through his stories of Uncle Remus, who told of

Brer Rabbit, Brer Fox, and other trickster figures who intimated the dark side of slavery and formulas for survival. They were reflections of African American folklore, if filtered through a white southerner's imagination. Uncle Remus told entertaining tales to a young white lad, but beneath the surface was a subtext of violence and interracial strife. Harris raised what would be a recurring concern about white southerners' appropriating aspects of African American creativity for their own benefit, a concern balanced by Harris's acknowledgment and appreciation of black folk sources for his stories. Some of the tales came out of European and Native American lore as well.

Another local colorist, African American writer Charles Waddell Chesnutt, grew up in Fayetteville, North Carolina, to which he returned after working in the North, and began writing about African American life in a white-dominated world. *The Conjure Woman* (1899) featured former slaves as dialect-speaking narrators who assumed a humorous pose to disguise their subversive view of southern plantation life. His other novels probed black folk culture and history and contributed a realistic counternarrative to the dominant romanticized southern literature of the era.

Modernism

The South was slow to modernize, but by the 1920s southern writers were incorporating aspects of modernism into their works, albeit often in rural and small-town settings. Moving away from Victorian certainties, many southern writers explored such typical modernist themes as alienation, uncertainty, fragmentation, and marginality. *I'll Take My Stand: The South and the Agrarian Tradition* (1930) collected the essays of writers, mostly associated with Vanderbilt University, who defended agrarianism as the southern tradition worth preserving. They exemplified the region's role as a critical intellectual counterforce to the disruptions of modernity, offering a critique of industrialism's dark underside.

But the volume was altogether defensive in tone, launched a continuing narrative of loss and limitation, and, most important, denied African Americans a central role in southern culture. However, modernist writers, including the agrarians, represented a generational rebellion against the older South they had inherited, with little use for the genteel old-money southern aristocracy.

Southern modernism also embraced sociological realism, emphasizing the social and cultural significance of the plain folk, the yeoman origins of planters, the leveling effects of the frontier, and the pervasiveness of egalitarian ideals. Erskine Caldwell, in his popular novels and nonfiction, showed a South that had gone to hell in the dysfunctional sharecropping and mill-town economy. He became the South's best-selling novelist, with 25 novels and 150 short stories over a forty-year career. The documentary genre emerged in the 1930s, using field research that combined photography and writers' observations and reflections and gave voice to the poor and suffering people of the rural South in the depression. James Agee and Walker Evans's *Let Us Now Praise Famous Men* (1941) came out of their time living in Alabama and told a story of their poverty-stricken lives that Agee and Evans invested with humane understanding. The federal government's Farm Security Administration and Works Progress Administration captured the voices and images of the South's people before the dramatic changes in the region in the 1940s.

William Faulkner emerged from rural and small-town north Mississippi to become the most acclaimed southern writer and winner of the Nobel Prize in 1950. Faulkner had tramped around Europe in the 1920s and had lived a bohemian life in New Orleans, but his writing did not flourish until he followed Sherwood Anderson's advice to go back to Oxford and write about the fictional Yoknapatawpha County. Family tales, local legends, and Mississippi history gave him the materials to create an imaginative world with tragedy and comedy. Self-taught and well read, he followed James Joyce's stylistic experimentations and mastered them, and he used contemporary understandings of human psychology in creating his characters.

The burdens of southern history preoccupied the Mississippian, and Faulkner portrayed the South's obsessions with the Civil War, the legend of Reconstruction, the decline of the antebellum plantation class, and the rise of working-class whites into bourgeois respectability and wealth. He could be romantic in his portrayal of glamorous Confederate leaders, but his tone was more likely to be gothic, with tales of a shadowy past, the never-ending influence of that past into the future, the cursed land, and doomed people. Dispossession of Indian land became the region's original sin, and white injustice toward blacks was the recurring theme. Faulkner's engagement with racial issues, his portrayals of primitive peasants, and the movement from rural areas to small towns all connected his work with other societies that suffered from industrialism, nationalism, and other broad global forces that had local impact.

Critics have rarely seen Margaret Mitchell as a major writer within southern modernism, but her achievement is apparent in producing the most popular literary work about the South. *Gone with the Wind* (1936) sold a million copies the year of its publication, and David O. Selznick's 1939 film created an extravagant visual version of Mitchell's story that updated the plantation novel and showed, more broadly, the close relationship between southern literary expressiveness and its translation into film. Mitchell, who in some ways honored the conventions of earlier southern writing, also was a modernist who was subversive of them through such unsentimental figures as Scarlett O'Hara and Rhett Butler. To be sure, portrayals of African Americans do not escape stereotyping, and the novel's racial ideology is fraught indeed.

Richard Wright came out of an oppressive Jim Crow childhood in Mississippi to author some of the most important works of southern modernism, at the forefront of protest by African American writers against racial injustice. Wright's memoir *Black Boy* (1945) recounted daily humiliation, physical and psychological danger, and downright hunger, both material and spiritual. As a teenager, Wright managed to check out library books, including those by the southern critic H. L. Mencken, that fired his imagination. Wright fled the South, but it continued to obsess him. His novel *Native Son* (1940) portrayed a young black migrant from the South who found the North far from the old Promised Land image. Zora Neale Hurston represented a different approach, one that celebrated black life in the South. She saw rural black folk culture nurturing a strong African American community. Growing up in an all-black town in Florida, Hurston became an anthropologist and documented the folk culture she celebrated in four novels, including *Jonah's Gourd Vine* (1934) and *Their Eyes Were Watching God* (1937).

Hurston had been a major figure in the Harlem Renaissance, which had emerged in the 1920s as part of the declaration of the New Negro as a creative American force and which paralleled the outpouring of southern modernist writing in the coming decades. Southern-born writers were a major part of the movement, and southern characters and settings represented a creative southern focus for Harlem Renaissance writers. Responding to the dynamic forces of economic change, social movement, and new opportunities as part of an urban civilization, African American writers looked back to the southern folk culture as a source of the meaning and identity that was the overarching aim of black writing in the period. Jean Toomer's *Cane* (1923) used a montage of poems, short stories, and sketches in good fragmented modernist style. Born in Washington, DC, Toomer spent three months as the principal of an African American school in rural Georgia, and he identified with country people whom he had met. The first part of the book painted a lyrical portrait of the southern landscape and black folk culture, albeit one filled with violence. The second part of the book explored black life in the urban North, with none of the beauty or the brutalities of southern black life. Sterling Brown's poetry collection *Southern Road* (1932) mythologized black laborers he had seen at work in the countryside, and one cycle of poems portrayed a trickster figure moving about between Arkansas, Atlanta, and Hell.

Born in Louisiana and raised in California, Arna Bontemps also became a poet when he moved to Harlem in the early 1920s and became identified with the Harlem Renaissance. Returning south, he served as a librarian at Fisk University in Nashville, Tennessee, the leading institution that researched and taught about black life in the South. His realistic short stories and novels showed the violence but also the joys of people in the countryside. *Black Thunder* (1936) displayed his interest in history, as he recounted a slave uprising, and he penned biographies of such African American heroes as Frederick Douglass and scientist George Washington Carver. He edited blues composer W. C. Handy's autobiography and coedited, with poet Langston Hughes, *The Book of Negro Folklore* (1958). His prolific work displayed the breadth of African American literature focused on its southern context.

Postsouthernist writing

The writers after 1980 lived in a different world than the past-haunted society that had given birth to the creative outpouring of earlier twentieth-century southern writing. A new term, *postsouthernism*, became a descriptor for writers living in the most economically prosperous and racially integrated South ever. These writers lived in a place that shared in the anxiety and concern for the authentic seen in late capitalist cultures.

Walker Percy was from one of Mississippi's most prominent families, but he was also a Catholic existentialist writer who probed the angst of modern life. His characters journeyed through the ruins of a prosperous modern South that had become a case study of spiritual maladies of a technological society. Critics see Percy's early novel *The Moviegoer* (1961) as perhaps the first postsouthern novel. Set in New Orleans, the novel follows its main character, Binx Bolling, as he rejects his family's elite past and chooses to live in suburban Gentilly, rather than the upscale old neighborhoods of the French Quarter and the Garden District. Bolling sees the increasing standardization around him and tries to make sense of the seeming absurdities of middle-class, consumer-driven, commodified culture, one that is a southern variant of larger national trends.

Self-conscious writers from the white working class, who seldom had appeared in literature as other than stereotypes, have become among the region's most acclaimed authors. Harry Crews was the progenitor of this trend; his memoir *A Childhood: The Biography of a Place* (1978) portrayed the rough South of his family life as they moved from sharecropping into the demanding industrial economy of south Georgia and north Florida. Other rough South writers portray the grittiness, violence, economic despair, and dysfunctional families, as well as humor, of working-class and poor white life. Crews mentored another writer from a background similar to his—Larry Brown, who grew up in Faulkner's county, Lafayette County, Mississippi. Brown was a country boy who worked hard on his father's sharecropping farm, hunted the woods and fished the rivers, but also read widely thanks to his mother. *The Iliad* and *The Odyssey* got him interested in mythology as a boy. He worked a series of jobs, which provided raw materials for his stories of people who set out pine trees, cut pulpwood, clean carpets, and bag groceries. Brown once observed that he wrote "about people surviving, about people proceeding out of calamity." They seemed lost but they were "aware of their need for redemption."

Although much white working-class writing portrays a rough South indeed, another writer, Janisse Ray, tells an upbeat story of her life's experiences, despite growing up in poverty. Her memoir, *Ecology of a Cracker Childhood* (1999), tells of life in a junkyard in south Georgia, surrounded by hulks of old cars and stacks of blown-out tires. To be sure, most people she knew "worried about getting by," but she recalls constantly being reminded of blessings in her childhood: "health, enough food, a place to live, parents who loved us beyond reasons." Her grandfather taught her to love the woods, and her compassionate father showed her how to care for animals and people. "I was a Southerner," she declares, a white working-class version of that identity that included a passionate environmental outlook.

African American writers continue to place their stories in the southern context where the land, environment, family, folklore, religion, and language matter. They often build on the memory of the civil rights movement to address continuing inequalities in the region. Ernest J. Gaines's *The Autobiography of Miss Jane Pittman* (1971) is an iconic exploration of a central figure who lived through dramatic times in African American history from the Civil War to the civil rights movement. Gaines, who was raised on a plantation in Oscar, Louisiana, before his family left for California, created a memorable southern landscape called St. Raphael Parish, with African Americans, Cajuns, Creoles, and white farmers.

Natasha Trethewey, who won the Pulitzer Prize for poetry in 2007 and was named the nation's poet laureate in 2012, was born to interracial parents in Mississippi, and her poetry unravels the South's mixed-race heritage through poems about her own family's experiences. She reimagines southern history, with women and black people as central figures. Her 2002 sonnet "Southern Pastoral" pictures her in the nonpastoral black metropolis of Atlanta, having a drink with the all-white, all-male agrarian writers of the past. Randall Kenan used his childhood memories, growing up in a small North Carolina town that became the basis for his fictional Tim's Creek, where characters recur throughout many stories. In his short-story collection *Let the Dead Bury Their Dead* (1992), he draws from rural black folk culture, and his magical realism stories include African lore, ghosts, and haunted memories. He writes of gay characters who often cross racial lines.

Increasingly, writers from a variety of social and ethnic perspectives are producing works that show the changing demography of the South. Robert Olen Butler writes of Vietnamese in Louisiana in *A Good Scent from a Strange Mountain* (1992) and how their memories of war—the Vietnam War, not the Civil War—shape the lives of these new southerners. Susan Choi's *The Foreign Student* (1998) explores a protagonist haunted by his childhood during the Korean War, as well as his embrace of southern small-town life. If the South's new immigration is producing writers that chronicle it, the oldest southern residents are also producing accomplished writers who draw from native tribal history and contemporary Indian life with southern settings, including LeAnne Howe (Choctaw), James Harris Guy (Chickasaw), and Diane Glancy (Cherokee).

Writers who have claimed a lesbian and gay identity since the 1980s explore the region's complex attitudes toward homosexuality, making that identity part of a multicultural region but showing pushback from homophobic attitudes as well. Alice Walker's *The Color Purple* (1982) showed same-sex relationships and subversive figures who did not abide by traditional gender roles in a story set in the rural South of Depression times. Dorothy Allison's characters are from the rough working-class South, and she positions lesbian identities in a world of class struggle, child abuse, sexual abuse, and feminism. Her novel *Bastard out of Carolina* (1992) opens up a woman's world of young Bone Boatwright and her aunts. They are on the margins of the small-town South, poor and given low expectations by their society and families. Bone's Aunt Raylene is a lesbian who is independent and free from male patriarchal demands. If Allison is deadly serious in her examination of lesbianism in the rough South, Fannie Flagg, in her novel *Fried Green Tomatoes at the Whistle Stop Café* (1987), uses humor in suggesting a love relationship between two women, showing a tolerant community, as the women welcomed all comers in a free atmosphere surprisingly set in the small-town South.

Southern writers in the early twenty-first century have lived in a very different society than those who grew up in the region's long-dominant rural and small-town places. They still claim identities as southern, although those identities are more varied than ever. Globalization has added new economic and cultural dimensions to the region's society, and writers reflect that development. Southern literature has, in fact, long explored transnational perspectives, including Zora Neale Hurston's stories of Haiti and William Faulkner's *Absalom, Absalom!*, whose plot turns on the planter Thomas Sutpen's time in the Caribbean. Latin American writers, in turn, have been drawn to southern writers. It was appropriate that Nobel Prize–winning author Gabriel Garcia Marquez slipped quietly into Oxford, Mississippi, in the 1980s to pay homage to Nobel laureate Faulkner. As part of the visit, he went to Faulkner's grave and, in a gesture the whiskey-loving Mississippian would have hailed, poured bourbon on it.

Chapter 7
Hybrid sounds

Bob Wills & His Texas Playboys roamed the Southwest of Texas and Oklahoma before World War II and then Southern California after the war, playing a joyous music that they called western swing. Although called "western," it exemplified the cross-fertilization that has made the American South a place well known as part of the global jukebox and points to the significance of music in the overall southern story. Wills's sound joined two strains of culture in the South, one white and one black. It combined the fiddle music typical of rural life throughout the Southeast with the jazz syncopation, blues feelings, and scat singing more identified with African American music than country music. His swinging rhythms could be those of big-band popular music, but they were also well rooted in country vernacular styles.

Wills often recorded songs that referenced the South, none more memorably than "That's What I Like about the South." Its lyrics dwelled on food as what the narrator liked about the region, including baked ribs and candied yams, sugar-cured Virginia hams, hot cornbread, and black-eyed peas. "Won't you come with me to Alabamy?" opens the song, with the singer remembering his "dear old Mammy" who was "fryin' eggs and cooking hammy." It ends with an invitation for listeners to go "Down where they say, 'Y'all' / Walk on in with that Southern drawl." Southern music, including that of Wills, tells much about the cultural representations and processes that constructed a southern identity.

Long before Bob Wills, American culture had come to picture the South as either barbaric or romantic, but with exotic, singing people, white and black, as part of the scene. Musical southerners indeed often sang of the hills of old Virginia, or the plains of Texas, or the crossroads of the Mississippi delta, marking specific places as "southern" places and constructing the geography of the southern and American imagination. Images of cotton fields, lazy rivers, smoky mountains, lonesome pines, rambling men, pistol-packing women, loving mothers and fathers, beloved mountain cabins, jumping honky-tonks and juke joints, and heaven-bound railroads have reverberated through southern culture and shaped national perceptions of a South where people are just a bit different than the supposed national middle-class norms, past and present.

Southern music as a concept came from the work of academic researchers and record marketers. The concept drew on such regional connections as the accents and dialects of performers, country lifestyles and biographical narratives of musicians, performance styles that observers termed southern, and self-conscious regional identities seen in such song titles as "My Window Faces the South," "Southern Nights," and "If Heaven Ain't a Lot Like Dixie, I Don't Want to Go." The origins of southern music lie in Africa, Europe, and England, whose musical forms evolved on the American frontier, within the folk context of often-isolated southern rural areas. A common body of songs and instrumentation resulted that reflected the basic biracial interaction of the region's predominant populations from West Africa and western Europe. Africans, for example, brought the banjo from Africa and it became a slave musical instrument, but whites around them discovered it, so it became important in country music. White religious people with English backgrounds sang Dr. Watts's hymns at frontier biracial camp meetings, and they entered into slave repertoires. Commercialization was a factor as well: whites played the guitar, but when the Sears, Roebuck catalogue started advertising that instrument, African Americans ordered it and made it part of many African American–derived styles.

The folk context in the South also included contributions from Cajuns in south Louisiana, Czechs and Poles in central Texas, Germans in the Shenandoah valley, and Mexicans in south Texas. Cajun music was a mix of country, popular, and blues music. French-speaking African Americans who lived near Cajuns in southwest Louisiana created another fusion music, Zydeco, with Cajun sounds and rhythm and blues, all delivered with hybrid French–English lyrics. Tex-Mex music often included Spanish lyrics, instrumentation that included accordions, and performers who had an identifiable Latino audience but who also—like Johnny Rodriguez, Freddy Fender, and Tish Hinojosa—crossed over into country music. The line between folk and popular music was always a thin one, as musicians in the supposedly isolated southern rural areas borrowed from high art and popular music. The square dance so identified with country music came from the cotillion seen at plantation balls, and the cakewalk of black folk parodied formal white dancing. Cherished fiddle tunes among white performers, such as "Under the Double Eagle," came from marches and popular songs.

The nineteenth century

The first association of music with the American South came from the presence of African American slaves. Slave traders, captains of ships sailing from Africa, slave owners, travelers through the South—all commented on the propensity of black people in the South to sing, either sad laments from the fields or joyous spirituals from the slave quarters, linking this musicality to the plantation. W. E. B. Du Bois, in *The Souls of Black Folk* (1903),

10. The fiddle has been associated with southern music from early in colonial history. It came as the violin from the European high-art tradition, but it entered folk culture as an accessible instrument that came to be especially associated with rural white culture. African Americans played it as well, as William R. Ferris portrayed in this photograph of Tom Dumas at his home in the Mississippi delta in 1967.

affirmed that African American religious music from slave times was "the most original and beautiful expressions of human life and longing yet born on American soil."

The pre–Civil War minstrel show displayed southern connections in its imagery of the plantation. Early minstrel performers were often from the Midwest, not the South, but they had traveled in the Mississippi River valley and heard slaves at work. They portrayed life on the plantations in romanticized ways that defenders of slavery would have endorsed, with singing slaves reifying the proslavery mantra of happy-go-lucky enslaved workers. These entertainers were usually white people corked up in blackface, establishing a demeaning masked representation for African Americans that would long endure in American culture.

The blackface minstrel shows were important, however, in the development of southern music because they introduced songs, dance forms, comedy routines, vocal styles, and instrumentation that southerners long preserved and came to think of as indigenous to the region. The late nineteenth century saw new forms of traveling shows that contributed tunes and instrumentation that entered the folk process in southern communities. White listeners heard African American musicians on street corners, in work gangs, and at public gatherings. They eavesdropped on black people singing in church worship services and at funerals and revivals. Jerry Lee Lewis was not the only white musician who went to black juke joints and picked up the piano sounds he heard there. Black servants heard the music of white people in the homes they cleaned and among the people for whom they cooked, and African Americans heard white performers at public venues, on the radio, and on recordings.

After emancipation, African Americans gained employment in such groups as the Georgia Minstrels as they moved to New Orleans, Memphis, and St. Louis, where they adopted the trumpet, the piano, and other instruments that soon became familiar in the music of black southerners. Sacred music remained central to evolving forms of that music. Spirituals had been one of the most defining features of slave culture, songs of praise and sorrow that grew out of the trauma of slavery and loss of African religious systems and reflected the conversion of African Americans to the promises of Christian faith.

Commercializing African American music

Scott Joplin converted rag rhythms to classical forms in the hit song "Maple Leaf Rag" (1900) and helped create a new popular, piano-based music that came to be called ragtime. Joplin was African American, but white musicians soon adopted the style. Closely related to ragtime was jazz. The Original Dixieland Jass Band, a white group in New Orleans, was the first southern jazz group to record, in 1915. Bandleader King Oliver was also from New Orleans, and his group was the first African American jazz band to record, but not until 1923. In the early twentieth century, New Orleans, with its Storyville neighborhood, was home to bordellos, saloons, and strip clubs, all of which employed jazz performers and helped popularize the music within the city. Grim poverty was often behind the drive of early jazz performers, but the city's relatively easygoing ways, cosmopolitan port-city outlook, and Spanish and French influences provided a context for its people to appreciate a music rooted in improvisation and cultural fusion. The African influence was undeniable, with jazz origins in the music and dancing at Congo Square going far back in southern history.

Brass bands had long been in the city and provided foundational sounds for the music as well, along with barrelhouse pianos common in entertainment districts. Buddy Bolden became the preeminent jazzman in the early twentieth century, combining brass band sounds with blues notes. By the mid-1920s, jazz was popular nationally and internationally, the soundtrack to the Roaring Twenties. Louis Armstrong's popularity made him an icon of jazz and its southern roots. Mardi Gras, the Jazz Festival, and the Preservation Hall made New Orleans of continuing importance to jazz, even though the music moved north after the 1930s and evolved into new forms.

Blues music grew out of hard lives in the rural South, among poor, mostly uneducated, and musically untrained African Americans on the plantations of the Mississippi delta and in such heavy-labor industries as logging, mining, and levee and railroad construction. Early music depicting black American lives had been stereotypical, whether in minstrelsy or the "coon songs," with their demeaning images, but in the late nineteenth century the blues form emerged in the South itself, out of work songs and chants. This new music reflected a realistic perspective on everyday life, especially relationships between men and women, but also portrayed current events, natural disasters, migration, alcohol and drugs, and racial discrimination.

Local places mattered. The thumping bass rhythms of Blind Lemon Jefferson, an iconic figure in east Texas blues, were different from the lyrically and rhythmically intense Delta blues, and the Carolina Piedmont produced a still-different, lighter, bouncier sound. In the early twentieth century, professional itinerant musicians incorporated blues sounds into their repertories in cities and towns. W. C. Handy heard the mournful sounds of the blues at Tutwiler, near Clarksdale, Mississippi, and he soon became a leading composer of blues songs that entered the world of commercial American music. In the 1920s, phonograph records and radio helped popularize the blues, including such "blues queens" as Ma Rainey, Bessie Smith, and Clara Smith, and country blues performers including Charley Patton from the Delta and Blind Willie McTell from Georgia. Robert Johnson became a mysterious figure who evoked some of the darkest moods of the blues in songs like "Hellhound on My Trail," which gave poetic evocation to the traumas of postemancipation African American life. The legend of Johnson selling his soul to the Devil at the Delta crossroads has been an enduring story, although musicologists now see Johnson not as a mystical singer carrying the burden of African spiritual ways with the crossroads dating back to Africa, but rather as a modern entertainer who worked for commercial success.

The growing influence of jazz and the appearance of electric guitars by the 1940s, along with the migration of African Americans northward, made Chicago and other northern cities new centers of blues culture, represented by the big sounds of Muddy Waters (McKinley Morganfield) and Howlin' Wolf (Chester Burnett), and later Texan Aaron "T-Bone" Walker and Mississippi's B. B. King. Blues would influence such country music legends as Jimmie Rodgers and Hank Williams; it also shaped rock 'n' roll, including white performers like Elvis Presley in the early days, the Rolling Stones and the Beatles in the 1960s, and some southern rock groups in the 1970s.

Country music

Like blues music, the predominantly white folk music that became country music was in its origins the sounds of the working class, centered, like the blues, in rural and small-town southern life. Musicologists and folklorists began documenting this music around the turn of the twentieth century, as Cecil Sharp scoured the Appalachian Mountains for the purest forms of English ballads and John Lomax recorded the songs of cowboys in the Southwest and prisoners and others in the Deep South. The 1920s brought local radio stations that played this music, and the decade saw talent scouts coming into the South for the recording and marketing of "hillbilly" music (as distinct from African American music, which record companies categorized as "race" music). This hillbilly music did not fit the folklorists' profile, however, because it was by no means a pure Anglo-American cultural form as they had thought, but rather an ethnically and racially hybrid sound, affected by commercialization and new technologies.

Jimmie Rodgers became the "Father of Country Music" and influenced generations of performers. His mother died young, and relatives raised him in towns across the Deep South, with Meridian, Mississippi, becoming his home. He was a touring musician, a songster like many early bluesmen, who worked in carnivals, tent shows, circuses, and minstrel shows. Mobile and restless, he worked on the railroads, whose lore he incorporated into his songs. Rodgers is a prime example of the cultural interaction of white and black musicians, as he sang white blues, recorded with Louis Armstrong, and, in turn, appealed to such black blues performers as Howlin' Wolf.

The Depression and World War II saw momentous changes as new genres of country music appeared, including western swing in the Southwest; honky-tonk sounds centered in the places where the white working classes now toiled in industrial jobs at factories and in oil fields; and the hard-driving bluegrass sound created by Bill Monroe. Expanded audiences in areas outside the South, as well as roles in western films, brought new performance opportunities and gave birth to the new label "country and western." Nashville, Tennessee, became the commercial and cultural center of the music; the Grand Ole Opry staged radio broadcasts by the 1930s and major record companies established studios along the city's Music Row.

In the 1950s, new sounds began to appear, including the lush, well-orchestrated Nashville Sound that sought to cross over to mainstream popular music. The 1970s saw the emergence of the Austin scene of Willie Nelson and the long-running television show "Austin City Limits," as well as the outlaw movement that brought together performers seeking economic and cultural independence from the Nashville music establishment. Meanwhile, generations of new popular performers took the music away from its rural roots and traditional fiddle and steel-guitar sounds with blander sounds to appeal to new suburban and broader national audiences—leading, in turn, to periodic reassertion of roots music and country revival performers who sought to recapture the original music's appeal.

Religious music

Sacred music was an early part of southern white folk culture, as well as among African Americans in the region. Church people in the early nineteenth century sang old British hymns and carols and the evangelical songs of Methodist writers such as Charles Wesley and John Newton. Camp meetings saw new melodies appear. Songs circulated in shape-note form, a form of notation in which the shape of the note indicated its musical pitch—*fa* was a triangle, *la* a square, and *mi* a diamond. Singing schools served as training grounds for shape-note teachers, who spread through the countryside, and tune books such as the *Sacred Harp* and *Southern Harmony* provided a musical repertoire for religious singing, public and private. Early nineteenth-century black southerners sang not only the distinctive spirituals but also camp meeting songs and Protestant hymns learned from missionaries.

The late nineteenth century saw gospel music become the new name for music defined by the 1870s in the publications of Ira Sankey, song leader for the era's leading revivalist, Dwight Moody. Paperback hymnals published these songs in shape-note form, enabling people in country churches to sing them and becoming notable in a southern religious–musical ritual—the weekend singing conventions that became legendary as the "all-day-singings with dinner on the grounds." Often sentimental and nostalgic, the songs pictured country churches, family hearths, and spiritually nurturing mothers but, above all, a comforting Jesus, helping to create intimate possibilities for singers to know the love of Jesus. "What a Friend We Have in Jesus," "Washed in the Blood of the Lamb," and "In the Garden" are typical.

Pentecostal and Holiness churches became important new sources of religious traditions in the early twentieth century, and they embraced these tunes. This charismatic tradition began as attempts to restore a Wesleyan piety to the Methodist Church and stressed a religion of the heart that was open to emotional appeals and stirring music. Pentecostal and Holiness people moved beyond the traditional church piano and organ and embraced tambourines, horns, and electric guitars. Pentecostal and Holiness composers wrote such classic gospel songs as "When the Saints Go Marching In" and "Great Speckled Bird." The performance style of much modern black gospel music originated among African American Pentecostals in Memphis in the first decade of the twentieth century. Worshippers attending the Church of God in Christ, a predominantly black Pentecostal group whose headquarters was in the city, swayed with rhythmic intensity, including clapping of hands, shaking of heads, and shouted interpolations.

Black gospel was rooted in the sounds of the slave spirituals, blues performance styles, and ragtime piano influences, while white gospel came out of camp-meeting songs of the early nineteenth century, sacred harp singings, and revival music. Southerners pioneered with a variety of black gospel styles, such as solo performers in the mold of Mahalia Jackson (New Orleans) and Sister Rosetta Tharpe (Arkansas); guitar-accompanied blues–gospel singers (Blind Willie Johnson); half-spoken, half-sung preacher sermons; local church choirs; and interdenominational church choirs. Similarly, white gospel appeared in sacred songs sung on local radio stations, in church choirs, in package shows where promoters put together long concerts with a variety of religious singers, and through the inclusion of religious songs in such country music venues as radio's Grand Ole Opry. Gospel quartets long dominated religious performance among both black and white southerners, with Mississippi's Blackwood Brothers and South Carolina's Dixie Hummingbirds among the most popular. Both styles made a major impact on early rock 'n' roll performers in the region.

Rock 'n' roll

The early rock 'n' roll that appeared in southern places after World War II took root in cities, where the proximity of black and white performers in less constrained social relations than in the countryside encouraged cross-racial musical synthesis. Urban areas became the home for the new musical styles of rhythm and blues, rockabilly, and soul in recording and performing centers in Macon, Georgia; Muscle Shoals, Alabama; and, above all, Memphis, Tennessee.

Sun Studios in Memphis was the creation of the white producer Sam Phillips, whose success with Mississippian Elvis Presley made Sun legendary. In July 1954, Presley recorded "That's All Right," written by bluesman Arthur "Big Boy" Crudup; on the other side of the 45-rpm release was "Blue Moon of Kentucky," one of bluegrass pioneer Bill Monroe's songs. This combination of white and black musical forms defined early southern rock 'n' roll. The date of the recording was significant, only a few months before the Supreme Court's *Brown v. Board of Education* decision, which set the South on the path toward ending segregation laws. Early rock music coming out of the South represented the reach of young people to breach the long racial separation.

To be sure, rock performers did not campaign to end racial segregation, but Presley's music and that of other rock pioneers worked toward that end. They were young performers who were cultural rebels against many established southern ways. Young whites after World War II initiated the increased musical integration of the South's biracial culture as they listened to the energetic and impassioned singing on transistor radios bringing black-influenced styles into their homes and on the jukeboxes in diners and drug stores where they spent time among their young peers. They went to see black entertainers in concerts and, eventually, in clubs.

Presley epitomized the rebellion. In the context of the 1950s, he seemed a wild outlaw, riding a motorcycle and wearing black leather jackets, a rebel against white middle-class convention. He was in baggy pants and oversized jackets, "zoot suit" fashions he purchased on Memphis's Beale Street, a symbolic center of Deep South black culture. When Scotty Moore, Presley's guitarist, first met him, he thought the singer's name and his "black shirt, pink pants with black stripes, white shoes and . . . greasy ducktail" must be "something out of science fiction." Some white people might indeed have thought the African American styles that Presley displayed were out of this world, but young people followed Presley and other rockers in embracing the fashions, mannerisms, and accents of African Americans as well as their music.

Ray Charles was one of the most important innovators of rock music. Born in Albany, Georgia, he became blind as a child, but he grew up around music, especially hearing it in church. "I Got a Woman," from 1955, was one of his most influential recordings. It began with horns and a piano sounding like it could have been in church, and his falsetto shrieks added a sound that had long reverberated in "Sanctified" southern churches—of those possessed by the Holy Spirit. One of Charles's contributions was to adapt songs from black gospel groups like the Pilgrim Travelers and the Caravans, preserving the spirit-filled, impassioned style but adding secular lyrics. He helped to define rhythm and blues and later soul music. Charles also made a major contribution to the synthesis of biracial southern music with his album, *Modern Sounds in Country and Western Music* (1962). It was daring at the time for a black entertainer to enter so intentionally a country music industry that had few black performers, but the record sold over 3 million copies, gave him a new audience among white middle-class listeners, and made it easier for future black performers like Charley Pride to become country entertainers.

The South has continued to produce new musical sounds rooted in the region's evolving life—hip-hop and rap now attract young

African Americans more than the blues, while contemporary country music has lost its traditional pedal–steel guitar and fiddle instrumentation and singers come from around the world as well as the South. Roots music still has new expressions, however, as with the Carolina Chocolate Drops, an interracial North Carolina group that reprises traditional southern music.

One of the most intriguing southern musicians is Tish Hinojosa, who epitomizes a multicultural country music that is rooted in the Southwest. Growing up in San Antonio but with deep family roots in Mexico and south Texas, she plays an original blend of country, folk, and cowboy songs in both Spanish and English. The result is a fresh hybrid genre, Anglo-Hispanic western country music. Her "Taos to Tennessee" tells of her love of northern New Mexico, with her back warmed by a "Western sky" with its "fiery setting sun." She is moving to Tennessee to pursue her music in Nashville, and the lyric hopes for "a starry southern night / To shine a trail from Taos to Tennessee." Although "Southern ways are new to me," she concludes, for "a song, it's where I want to be." The connection between music and the South continues to be renewed.

Chapter 8
Southern tastes

America Eats was a Depression-era project intended to document the role of cooking in American life. Using the model of the Works Progress Administration's state guidebooks, researchers investigated such regional dishes as Kentucky burgoo and South Carolina chicken bog, both slow-simmered stews that men typically cooked, oyster roasts in coastal North Carolina, Coca-Cola get-togethers in Georgia, Mississippi chitlins, and a feast at the Polk County Possum Club in Mena, Arkansas.

For essays in support of the project, Mississippi's Eudora Welty gathered high-styled recipes dating back to pre–Civil War times, including deviled eggs, beaten biscuits, and mint juleps. With tongue in cheek, she insisted that even Yankees could make the dishes: "Follow directions and success is assured." African American writer Zora Neale Hurston told of Florida's "Diddy-Wah-Diddy," an imaginary black American place, she wrote, "of no work and no worry for man and beast." Go there and you found that "the food is even already cooked," with a tasty abundance for all. "If a traveler gets hungry all he needs do is sit down on the curbstone and wait and soon he will hear something hollering: 'Eat me! Eat me! Eat me!'" Hurston portrays a procession of walking dishes. A roasted chicken arrives with a knife and fork already in its side for carving. A sweet potato pie pushes to get in front of the traveler. "Nobody can ever eat it all up," Hurston concludes. Welty and Hurston's accounts suggest a range of southern eating. Welty's visits to antebellum homes point to plantation life, a world of privilege and certain distinctive foods, still surviving in the modern South. Hurston's story drew from a traditional African American folk tale, using humor but with a pointed subtext of a hungry South, which had become even worse in the Depression than ever before.

Both writers connected food to the southern context. The sense of a particular southern *terroir*—the relationship of food to an environment—and its cuisine goes far back in southern history. New Englander Jeremiah Evarts, for example, traveled south in the 1820s and wrote of his amazement at the abundance of food in the Sea Islands off Georgia's coast. He observed that "how all these things could be cooked would puzzle a northern man." If Evarts saw this coastal food as not just coastal but also "southern," he went on to add that the slavery he saw in southern parts was "abject beyond my powers of description," including daily slave meals of "coarse and scanty" food.

Origins

Southern foodways go back to the Native American peoples who had established distinctive food traditions by the Mississippian period, 1000–1500 CE. Cherokee legend identifies the ancestral progenitor as a mother, Selu, who gave the gift of corn, which became a foundational ingredient of the southern diet in general. Native women's association with corn led them to become the South's first intensive farmers, so productive that their societies grew and became more centralized, but giving rise to social class and gender divisions in the process. Indian agriculture reflected profound understanding of farming processes, such as planting beans next to corn to offset the corn's nitrogen-depleting tendencies. The Indian diet included beans, potatoes, tomatoes, eggplant, peppers, and the foundational three foods: sweet potatoes, turnips, and cowpeas. Wild game, fish and shellfish, and harvested wild plums, nuts, and blackberries supplemented their diet, depending on the location of tribes. The Columbian Exchange brought European-originated food plants into the South as part of a complex commercial web. The peanut, for example, originated in Brazil, was brought during the slave trade to Africa, and then (with the African name *goober*) brought on slave ships back to Virginia in the New World.

European American and African American settlers on the southern frontier came to eat as Indians ate from what grew well in southern soils, heat, and plentiful rain, in a long growing season. They killed and ate buffalo meat until the animal became extinct, then moved on to black bears and deer. Wild turkey was abundant, as were rabbit, squirrels, raccoons, and opossums, which were often mixed together in the original southern one-pot stews. Yeomen whites raised poultry, and they already prized fried chicken in antebellum times. But King Corn and King Hog were the culinary equivalents of King Cotton in defining the antebellum South's culture. One might add King Whiskey as well, since southerners of all sorts consumed large quantities of it, once the Scots-Irish on the Upper South frontier figured out how to make the amber beverage from corn.

The term *Big Eating* leads to the plantation dining table and the defining legend of *southern hospitality* as far back as colonial Virginia. Historian Edmund Morgan referred to the "culinary sociability among white elites" there, with the table the "ritual center of Virginia hospitality." Travelers noted hospitality throughout early southern history, but with real limitations. A visitor well introduced could expect to be welcomed, but that was less so for a stranger, much less a working-class person who wandered onto plantation grounds. Hospitality fit into the southern romantic myth of the Cavalier origins of planters, which went back to remembered British images of gentility. Hospitality would come to transcend elite offerings, however, as African

Americans and yeomen whites in later times would cherish the "groaning table" and the church supper as welcoming occasions.

The household was the location of food production in the antebellum South, and the domestic economy depended on food. Planters' wives held the key to the larder, a source of her authority over servants, who planted vegetable gardens, tended livestock, preserved produce, cooked meals, and served whites at the table. Slave rations were modest and barely sufficient to enable the labor that produced the staple crops that delivered so much wealth to slave owners. They calculated the basics of food in the counting-house manner that was a reality of slave management. In slave narratives, African American voices from within the plantation household unveiled how slave owners used food to control and discipline slaves. Frederick Douglass contrasted the "substandard rations of slaves" with what he called the "blood-bought luxuries" of the planter family. Harriet Jacobs showed the meanness with which some plantation mistresses treated their slaves in terms of food supplies, recounting how one would spit in the leftovers from Sunday dinners so the slaves could not eat them.

The rural South, where most black Americans lived, nurtured distinctive African American foodways that went back to African methods of food preparation. These included boiling, toasting, or roasting, steaming in leaves, baking in the ashes of fires, and deep frying in oil—the latter becoming the epitome of the southern style of cooking. Indeed, slaves added their food preparation methods to those of England inherited by southern whites, as well as bringing such specific food plants brought from Africa as okra, black-eyed peas, and sesame seeds. The slave cook became a legendary plantation figure, reshaping and reinterpreting evolving southern foodways. James Hemings, raised as a slave at Thomas Jefferson's Monticello, became a French-trained chef who utilized the local produce from Jefferson's estate and cooked in the White House. After emancipation, whites came to rely on domestic servants, who would sometimes live in white households but more often came for the day to cook, care for children, or clean. They became known as "the help," in southern vernacular—making the household a central institution for the creation of an interracial cultural exchange, one unfair in its power relationships, sometimes harsh in its interactions, but at other times loving and caring around the essentials of food.

On the eve of the Civil War, one northern governess, Rogene Scott, who had come south to Kentucky from Vermont, noted the importance of material life, including food, to the residents south of the Mason–Dixon line. "The Southerner feels differently [than the northerner]; if he has a plenty to eat and drink and wear he scarcely thinks of anything else." Rather than criticizing this regional attitude, however, Scott embraced it, noting that she had "fallen greatly in love with my style of living because it is so simple and wholesome and I so perfectly satisfied with it." Defeat of the Confederacy in the Civil War brought impoverishment to the South, and the working classes bore the worst suffering.

Sharecropping and tenant farming became the new economic arrangement that left agricultural workers to purchase much of their food from exploitive plantation commissaries or country stores. Cornmeal and pork continued to be the mainstays of the southern diet, although the Midwest now milled the grain and grew and slaughtered many of the hogs that ended up on southern tables. The traditional food trinity of turnips, cowpeas, and sweet potatoes contributed valuable nutrition to those families who had land available for gardens (most landowners wanted to reserve every inch of land for growing staple crops for sale, thus depriving many sharecroppers of land for vegetables). Foodways that had begun generations earlier survived into the twentieth century throughout southern places, not only among sharecroppers but also among mill workers and townspeople. The noonday meal, known as *dinner*, was the main meal for most southerners, with shared preferences across racial lines for heavy meals of pork, peas, and greens (cooked in pork), washed down with buttermilk,

lemonade, or sweet tea and perhaps cobbler or chess pie
afterward. This diet, though it brought warm memories of home
to southerners, black and white, led to serious malnutrition.
Pellagra became a debilitating southern disease among southern
working classes, resulting from overreliance on a diet of what
became known as the "3Ms"—meal, meat, and molasses.
Midwestern milled corn had inadvertently removed a key
nutrient, niacin, resulting in pellagra. Scientific research
discovered the problem, and changes in milling processes to retain
niacin, in addition to changes in the overall southern diet in the
twentieth century, brought the disease to an end.

Such changes represented the modernization of southern
foodways, beginning in the early twentieth-century Progressive
Era. Wheat flour purchased from the Midwest enabled the
increased consumption of biscuits, which became a "modern" and
middle-class alternative to traditional cornbread. Food across the
South became more standardized, knitting the regions within the
South together more tightly. Canned goods and commercial "light"
bread made a difference for better-off families, purchased now
from chain stores, such as the first self-service grocery, the Piggly
Wiggly stores founded in Memphis. Food had social class
meanings, as in the contrast between the new-fangled bologna
that the children of middle-class townspeople brought for school
lunches and the country-ham sandwiches in dinner pails that
rural children consumed. Paying cash to buy bologna in a grocery
store was modern, a wealthy consumer privilege, and had more
status at that time than the old-fashioned cured ham that even
tenant farmers had.

Few artifacts are as useful for understanding southern foodways
as cookbooks. In 1724, Eliza Smith published the first cookbook in
the colonies, in Williamsburg, Virginia, an expression of English
recipes and techniques brought to the New World, but Mary
Randolph's *The Virginia Housewife* (1824) reflected the
appearance of recognizably southern cookery based in plantation

life. Her recipes became iconic, reflecting not only the inheritance of English cuisine but also the influence of Native American dishes and slave cooks bearing the imprint of Africa and the Caribbean. Malinda Russell's *A Domestic Cook Book* (1866) was the first cookbook by a black American, but Abby Fisher's *What Mrs. Fisher Knows about Old Southern Cooking* (1881) showed an ex-slave from South Carolina claiming rights to the inheritance of Old South cooking and the empowerment and modest wealth that could come from it in the late nineteenth-century years of nostalgia for the Old South.

Women authored most cookbooks, and they also made a vital contribution to twentieth-century southern foodways through the egg-and-butter money that rural farm women generated through home production for sale to local merchants, at weekly curb markets around courthouses or city halls, and to regular town customers. By the 1920s, female county extension agents assisted in organizing these exchanges, which became important social occasions and generated funds that enabled families to have some stability amid the vagaries of the staple-crop economy.

Beginning in the 1890s, a rising middle class of businessmen and women and a working class with cash enabled more southerners than ever to participate in the spectacle of shopping. Food became as well an important aspect of the tourism economy that expanded throughout the twentieth-century South, with home-and-travel magazines featuring the Lowcountry seafood of the Carolina coast, the Creole tastes of New Orleans, and the traditional dishes of mountain and hill country places.

Advertisers and merchants branded the Old South with romantic new appeal in consumer food culture that reflected memories of prewar plantation society, just as the South—and the nation—was less rural and agricultural than ever before. New food products appeared, including White Lily flour in Knoxville (1883), Coca-Cola in Atlanta (1886), Pepsi-Cola in New Bern, North Carolina

(1898), and Duke's mayonnaise in Greenville, South Carolina (1917), all touchstones of local food culture that were South-wide through distribution. Martha White flour of Nashville (1899) became affiliated with the country music South through regular advertisements on the Grand Ole Opry's radio show, complete with a catchy jingle that generations of southerners could sing as they reached for the flour sack.

The Dixie brand, whether on flour, coffee, or endless other products, summoned appealing images of the Old South plantation, like Mammy, the by-now glamorous Confederate leaders like Robert E. Lee (whose image appeared on a flour sack), and, in general, a rural, slower, more leisurely past, one in which whites owned black bodies and their labor. Aunt Jemima was the classic representation of the African American cook used to sell modern packaged food. Nancy Green was a former slave working in Chicago when the promoters of that city's World's Columbian Exposition in 1893 hired her to dress as the stereotypical Mammy, tell stories of the Old South, sing songs, and hawk the newly marketed Aunt Jemima pancake flour. The company soon trademarked the image and used it to sell to busy housewives who appreciated the convenience of a flour mix approved by the representation of the legendary slave cook.

The mid-twentieth century

After World War II, changes came to foodways in the South, thanks partly to the increased mobility during the war, the increased travel made possible by the interstate highway system, the reliance on refrigeration for wider food distribution, and booming postwar prosperity that eventually eroded material discrepancies between the long economically depressed South and other parts of the nation. "Eating out" was southern vernacular for the movement of cooking and eating out of the home to fancy, fine-dining restaurants in cities and to town square cafes, hamburger joints, catfish shacks, and fried chicken and barbecue stands. Fast-food chains (both national ones like McDonald's and southern-based franchises such as Kentucky Fried Chicken) sold not only traditional southern food but also the image of the region through the white-suited Colonel Harland Sanders's marketeering.

Southern laws required segregation in eating, reflecting the essential southern racist taboo against the races eating together. The emergence of a more prosperous African American middle class gave its members the money to eat out, and food-related protests became central to the civil rights movement in the 1950s and 1960s. During the Montgomery bus boycott of 1956–57, Georgia Theresa Gilmore, like other black women, fed protestors and raised money from her cooking to support the boycott, and her "back door" restaurant attracted white and black customers to keep her prosperous during the boycott. She continued to feed activists, including during the 1965 Selma-to-Montgomery march. Student sit-ins, which began in Greensboro, North Carolina, in 1960, took place at department store lunch counters, leading Woolworth's to end segregation in food service by the summer of that year.

Atlanta's black-owned Paschal's Restaurant was a meeting place for civil rights activists, where they could eat what Andrew Young called a "sacramental meal" of comfort food that "provided the energy and spirit that gave birth to freedom." But food was central to resistance to change as well. Pickrick Cafeteria in Atlanta, Maurice's Piggie Park in Columbia, South Carolina, and Ollie's Barbecue in Birmingham, all owned by white segregationists, refused to accept the civil rights laws that required desegregation of eating establishments. It was only the rulings of federal courts that forced them to accept the laws or close their businesses. The Pickrick closed, but Maurice's and Ollie's adapted to new clientele.

Hunger was a haunting underside to southern foodways throughout much of southern history, and it did not disappear, despite the growth of a more prosperous mid-twentieth-century South. African Americans suffered much from poverty, reflected in Richard Wright's harsh memories of food deprivation in his memoir *Black Boy* (1947), which he originally entitled *American Hunger*. In rural areas before modernization, the long growing season for subsistence farming cushioned the effects of economic hard times, but sharecropping could be devastating for food deprivation. The 1960s saw a new focus on poverty and hunger in the nation, dramatized by President Lyndon Johnson's trip to economically depressed eastern Kentucky in 1964, his subsequent War on Poverty, and the creation of school lunch programs.

Long-time freedom fighter Fannie Lou Hamer addressed rural southern hunger in the late 1960s and 1970s through a successful Pig Bank program that made piglets available to local Delta families who would produce and share their livestock herds. She helped initiate the cooperative farming movement as well. By the twenty-first century, hunger and malnutrition had decreased in the South. But they had not gone away, as they were found in such places outside the economic mainstream as Appalachia, the Mississippi delta, the Alabama Black Belt, Indian reservations, and urban inner cities. Obesity was the new expression of malnourishment, stemming from endemic problems, such as food deserts where nutritious, inexpensive foods could be hard to find, and the resultant consumption of high-calorie processed convenience store foods and sweet drinks. High rates of heart disease, hypertension, diabetes, and cancer resulted.

A food renaissance

Agribusiness has long been the predominant form of farming in the South. The production of corn spawned processed foods in the American diet and the industrial production of poultry and hogs under appalling conditions for the animals and workers who handled them. At the same time, the twenty-first century South is experiencing a food renaissance. Traditional southern foods are given an update, as with pecan-encrusted catfish and butter-bean crostini, and food magazines seek out older restaurants still serving meat-and-three-vegetable lunches or regional variations within the South of the iconic barbecue. But increased diversity is the most dramatic indicator of the importance of southern foodways to the contemporary South. Cookbook recipes show how Italian, Lebanese, Mexican, French, vegetarian, and other cuisines are intermingling in a new fusion food. Locally sourced and organic foods have a new cachet in the South, with farmers' markets, buying clubs, food cooperatives, health restaurants, natural food bakeries, and other institutions marketing a countercultural new southern way of eating. Strikingly, to many contemporary southerners the acronym CSA is less likely to stand for the Confederate States of America than for community-supported agriculture.

Chefs and food writers have become iconic figures in this southern food renaissance, which echoes the earlier flowering of literature and music. Bill Neal was one of the pioneers in this new food scene; he grew up on traditional southern cookery, but learned to use French techniques with the bounty of North Carolina farms in his watershed restaurants La Residence and Crook's Corner, in Chapel Hill. "I had to go abroad to appreciate the mystery of food and its rituals in my native southland," he wrote. *Bill Neal's Southern Cooking* (1985) was a landmark, and he and his many proteges helped to remake the southern food scene. Cookbook writer and television personality Nathalie Dupree published *New Southern Cooking* in 1986 and launched an influential public television cooking show that extended the audience for that cuisine. Mississippi's Craig Claiborne used the august position of food columnist for the *New York Times* to popularize the new food movement as well.

In January 2008, the African American chef Edna Lewis published an essay entitled "What Is Southern?" in *Gourmet* magazine. In its original draft, Lewis posed the question, "How did southern food come into being?" Noting that African Americans had done much of the early cooking in the region, she concluded that "what began as hard work became creative work." She further insisted that "there is something about the South that stimulates creativity in people, be they black or white writers, artists, cooks, builders, or primitives that pass away without knowing they were talented." She relished the southern environment, having grown up in the rural setting of a family farm in Freeport, Virginia, and she wrote of the connectedness between family members and the extended community who would gather for rituals like hog killings or corn shuckings. But "southern" to Lewis also included Bessie Smith, Bourbon Street and Louis Armstrong, Richard Wright, "a pig foot and a bottle of beer," and "fresh-made corn fritters, light and crisp enough to fly away." Hate was a part of her South, too, but she closed the essay with a reference to Martin Luther King Jr. and his dream of reconciliation.

This "manifesto" for a southern sense of place rested, to be sure, in Lewis's nostalgic memories of her family life and the possibilities for creativity given her. The granddaughter of slaves, Lewis became one of the most celebrated chefs in New York City in the 1940s and 1950s, working at the famed Café Nicholson. She brought to her essay, and to her cookbooks, *The Taste of Southern Cooking* (1983) and *The Gift of Southern Cooking: Recipes and Revelations from Two American Chefs* (2003), coauthored with Scott Peacock, the intellectual sophistication gained from her time in the metropolitan North. Her story, however, was one of how the best of southern traditional culture could thrive, even in the modern world. At the end of the essay, she noted that "the world has changed," that the rural society that had nurtured earlier creativity was long gone. But "we are now faced with picking up the pieces and trying to put them into shape, document them so the present-day young generation can see what southern food was like." That traditional food, she wrote, rested not on some purely nostalgic memory, but on such environmental foundations as "pure ingredients, open-pollinated seed—planted and replanted for generations—natural fertilizers." By the time she published the essay, Lewis had already become a model and inspiration for the contemporary South's chefs and cooks, farmers and artisanal craftspeople, heritage gardeners, food writers, editors, and academic food researchers all seeking to extend an abiding food creativity into the twenty-first century.

The southern food movement emerged from what had been the most unifying aspect of an often divisive southern culture, and its notably multiracial and diverse ethnic character seems to presage now a more inclusive southern identity that welcomes and even celebrates differences that are still called southern.

References

Introduction

Eugene Walter, *American Cooking: Southern Style* (New York: Time–Life Books, 1971), 8.

Chapter 1: Becoming southern

"Name of New Guinea," in "Colonel William Byrd on Slavery and Indented Servants, 1736, 1739," *American Historical Review* 1 (1895):88.

"Without law in the States," in Mary Young, "The Cherokee Nation: Mirror of the Republic," *American Quarterly* 33 (Winter 1981): 522.

Chapter 2: Section to nation

Alexander Stephens, in Drew Gilpin Faust, *Creation of Confederate Nationalism: Ideology and Identity in the Civil War South* (Baton Rouge: Louisiana State University Press, 1988), 101.

Chapter 3: Tradition and modernization

Arkansas sharecropper quoted in Jack Temple Kirby, *Rural Worlds Lost: The American South, 1920–1960* (Baton Rouge: Louisiana State University Press, 1987), 239.

Jump Jim Crow, in Newman Ivey White, *American Negro Folk-Songs* (Cambridge, MA: Harvard University Press, 1928), 8.

"Double consciousness," in W. E. B. Du Bois, *The Souls of Black Folk* (New York: Penguin Books, 1989), 3.

"Gonna leave this Jim Crow town," in Paul Oliver, *Blues Fell This Morning: The Meaning of the Blues* (New York: Horizon, 1960), 51.

Chapter 4: Confronting change

"Love our Constitution," in Thomas Brady, *Black Monday* (Jackson, MS: Citizens Councils of America, 1955), "Foreword," n.p.

"Respectable segregationists" quote in Neil R. McMillen, *The Citizens' Council: Organized Resistance to the Second Reconstruction, 1954–64* (Urbana: University of Illinois Press, 1971), 360.

"We are confronted with a moral issue," in Numan V. Bartley, *The New South, 1945–1980: The Story of the South's Modernization* (Baton Rouge: Louisiana State University Press and the Littlefield Fund for Southern History at the University of Texas, 1995), 338.

"An immense façade was beginning to crack," in Willie Morris, *Yazoo: Integration in a Deep-South Town* (New York: Harper's Magazine Press, 1971), 133.

"Sick and tired of being sick and tired," in Kay Mills, *This Little Light of Mine: The Life of Fannie Lou Hamer* (New York: Dutton, 1993), 108.

Chapter 6: Creative words

Jesmyn Ward quote in Laura M. Holson, "Marking Mississippi's Literary Trail from William Faulkner to Jesmyn Ward," *New York Times*, April 27, 2018, https://www.newyorktimes.com/2018/04/27/books-mississippi-faulkner-trail.html.

Faulkner quoted in Richard Gray, "Writing Southern Cultures," in *A Companion to the Literature and Culture of the American South*, ed. Richard Gray and Owen Robinson (Malden, MA: Blackwell, 2004), 11.

Son House quote, in David Evans, *Big Road Blues: Tradition and Creativity in the Folk Blues* (New York: Da Capo Press, 1982), 42–43.

Hurston quote, in Zora Neale Hurston, *Dust Tracks on the Road: An Autobiography* (1942; repr., Urbana: University of Illinois Press, 1984), 135.

"A cesspool of Baptists" and "a miasma of Methodists," in Susan
Ketchin, *The Christ-Haunted Landscape: Faith and Doubt in
Southern Fiction* (Jackson: University Press of Mississippi,
1994), 347.

"Childhood, in a very small Mississippi town," in *Faulkner in the
University: Class Conferences at the University of Virginia,
1957–1958*, ed. Frederick L. Gwynn and Joseph L. Blotner
(Charlottesville: University Press of Virginia, 1959), 41.

"It is good to be shifty in a new country" quote in Johnson Jones
Hooper, *Adventures of Captain Simon Suggs, Late of the
Tallapoosa Volunteers* (1844; repr., Chapel Hill: University of
North Carolina Press, 1969), 8.

Larry Brown quote in Susan Ketchin, *The Christ-Haunted Landscape:
Faith and Doubt in Southern Fiction* (Jackson: University Press of
Mississippi, 1994), 283.

Janisse Ray, *Ecology of a Cracker Childhood* (Minneapolis, MN:
Milkwood Editions, 1999), 30, 165.

Chapter 7: Hybrid sounds

W. E. B. Du Bois, *The Oxford W. E. B. Du Bois*, ed. Henry Louis Gates
Jr. (New York: Oxford University Press, 2014), 911.

Scotty Moore quoted in Peter Guralnick, *Last Train to Memphis: The
Rise of Elvis Presley* (Boston: Little, Brown, 1994), 91.

Tish Hinojosa, "Taos to Tennessee," Watermelon Records, 1992.

Chapter 8: Southern tastes

Eudora Welty, "Mississippi Eats," and Zora Neale Hurston, "Diddy-
Wah-Diddy," in *The Food of a Younger Land*, ed. Mark Kurlansky
(New York: Riverhead Books, 2009), 81–82, 101–9.

Evarts quote, in Marcie Cohen Ferris, *The Edible South: The Power of
Food and the Making of an American Region* (Chapel Hill:
University of North Carolina Press, 2014), 18.

Morgan quote, in Edmund Sears Morgan, *Virginians at Home:
Family Life in the Eighteenth Century* (Williamsburg, VA: Colonial
Williamsburg Foundation, 1952), 75.

Douglass quote, Frederick Douglass, *My Bondage and My Freedom*
(New York: Miller, Orton and Mulligan, 1855), 10.

Scott quote, in Ferris, *The Edible South*, 46–47.

"Sacramental meal," in Andrew Young, "Forward," to James Vaughan
Paschal, as told to Mae Armster Kendall, *Paschal: Living the
Dream: An Inspirational Memoir* (New York: iUniverse, 2006),
xvii, xviii.

Lewis quotes, in Edna Lewis, "What Is Southern," *Gourmet Magazine*
68 (January 2008): 24–30.

Further reading

Overviews

Boles, John B., ed. *A Companion to the American South*. Malden, MA: Blackwell, 2002.

Boles, John B. *The South through Time: A History of an American Region*. 3rd ed. Englewood Cliffs, NJ: Prentice Hall, 2004.

Brundage, W. Fitzhugh. *The Southern Past: A Clash of Race and Memory*. Cambridge, MA: Belknap Press of Harvard University Press, 2005.

Cobb, James C. *Away down South: A History of Southern Identity*. New York: Oxford University Press, 2005.

Flora, Joseph, and Lucinda Mackethan, eds. *The Companion to Southern Literature: Themes, Genres, Places, People, Movements, and Motifs*. Baton Rouge: Louisiana State University Press, 2002.

Gray, Richard, and Owen Robinson, eds. *A Companion to the Literature and Culture of the American South*. Malden, MA: Blackwell, 2004.

Early history

Berlin, Ira. *Many Thousands Gone: The First Two Centuries of Slavery in North America*. Cambridge, MA: Harvard University Press, 1998.

Fischer, David Hackett. *Albion's Seed: Four British Folkways in America*. New York: Oxford University Press, 1989.

Gomez, Michael A. *Exchanging Our Country Marks: The Transformation of African Identities in the Colonial and*

Antebellum South. Chapel Hill: University of North Carolina Press, 1998.

Heyrman, Christine Leigh. *Southern Cross: The Beginnings of the Bible Belt*. Chapel Hill: University of North Carolina Press, 1997.

Antebellum period

Barnes, L. Diane, Brian Schoen, and Frank Towers, eds. *The Old South's Modern Worlds: Slavery, Region, and Nation in the Age of Progress*. New York: Oxford University Press, 2011.

Censer, Jane Turner. *The Reconstruction of White Southern Womanhood*. Baton Rouge: Louisiana State University Press, 2003.

Faust, Drew Gilpin. *Mothers of Invention: Women of the Slaveholding South in the American Civil War*. New York: Vintage Press, 1996.

Foner, Eric. *Reconstruction: America's Unfinished Revolution, 1863–1877*. New York: Harper & Row, 1988.

Fox-Genovese, Elizabeth. *Within the Plantation Household: Black and White Women of the Old South*. Chapel Hill: University of North Carolina Press, 1988.

Goldfield, David R. *America Aflame: How the Civil War Created a Nation*. New York: Bloomsbury Press, 2011.

Johnson, Walter. *River of Dark Dreams: Slavery and Empire in the Cotton Kingdom*. Cambridge, MA: Belknap Press of Harvard University Press, 2013.

McCurry, Stephanie. *Masters of Small Worlds: Yeoman Households, Gender Relations, and the Political Culture of the Antebellum South Carolina Lowcountry*. New York: Oxford University Press, 1995.

McPherson, James M. *Battle Cry of Freedom: The Civil War Era*. New York: Oxford University Press, 1988.

Postbellum period

Ayers, Edward L. *The Promise of the New South after Reconstruction*. New York: Oxford University Press, 1992.

Beeby, James M. *Populism in the South Revisited: New Interpretations and Departures*. Jackson: University Press of Mississippi, 2012.

Blight, David. *Race and Reunion: The Civil War in American Memory*. Cambridge, MA: Belknap Press of Harvard University Press, 2001.

Hale, Grace Elizabeth. *Making Whiteness: The Culture of Segregation in the South, 1880–1940*. New York: Pantheon, 1998.

Hall, Jacquelyn Dowd, James L. Leloudis, Robert Rogers Korstad, Mary Murphy, Lu Ann Jones, Michael H. Frisch, and Christopher B. Daly. *Like a Family: The Making of a Southern Cotton Mill World*. Chapel Hill: University of North Carolina Press, 1987.

Harvey, Paul. *Freedom's Coming: Religious Culture and the Shaping of the South from the Civil War through the Civil Rights Era*. Chapel Hill: University of North Carolina Press, 2005.

Hunter, Tera W. *To 'Joy My Freedom: Southern Black Women's Lives and Labors after the Civil War*. Cambridge, MA: Harvard University Press, 1997.

Tullos, Allen. *Habits of Industry: White Culture and the Transformation of the Carolina Piedmont*. Chapel Hill: University of North Carolina Press, 1989.

Williamson, Joel. *The Crucible of Race: Black–White Relations in the American South since Emancipation*. New York: Oxford University Press, 1984.

Early twentieth century

Gilmore, Glenda Elizabeth. *Gender and Jim Crow: Women and the Politics of White Supremacy in North Carolina, 1896–1920*. Chapel Hill: University of North Carolina Press, 1996.

Hale, Grace Elizabeth. *Making Whiteness: The Culture of Segregation in the South, 1880–1940*. New York: Pantheon, 1998.

Kirby, Jack Temple. *Rural Worlds Lost: The American South, 1920–1960*. Baton Rouge: Louisiana State University Press, 1987.

Link, William. *The Paradox of Progressivism, 1880–1930*. Chapel Hill: University of North Carolina Press, 1992.

Tindall, George Brown. *The Emergence of the New South, 1913–1945*. Baton Rouge: Louisiana State University Press, 1967.

Wilkerson, Isabel. *The Warmth of Other Suns: The Epic Story of America's Great Migration*. New York: Vintage, 2011.

Civil rights and economic change

Bartley, Numan. *The New South, 1945–1980*. Baton Rouge: Louisiana State University Press, 1995.

Branch, Taylor. *Pillar of Fire: America in the King Years, 1963–65*. New York: Simon & Schuster, 1998.

Carter, Dan T. *The Politics of Rage: George Wallace, the Origins of the New Conservatism, and the Transformation of American Politics.* New York: Simon & Schuster, 1995.

Daniel, Pete. *Lost Revolutions: The South in the 1950s.* Chapel Hill: University of North Carolina Press, 2000.

Dittmer, John. *Local People: The Struggle for Civil Rights in Mississippi.* Jackson: University Press of Mississippi, 1994.

Eagles, Charles W. *The Price of Defiance: James Meredith and the Integration of Old Miss.* Chapel Hill: University of North Carolina Press, 2009.

Fredrickson, Kari A. *Cold War Dixie: Militarization and Modernization in the American South.* Athens: University of Georgia Press, 2013.

Garrow, David J. *Bearing the Cross: Martin Luther King Jr. and the Southern Christian Leadership Conference.* New York: Vintage, 1986.

Schulman, Bruce J. *From Cotton Belt to Sunbelt: Federal Policy, Economic Development, and the Transformation of the South, 1938–1980.* New York: Oxford University Press, 1991.

Sokol, Jason. *There Goes My Everything: White Southerners in the Age of Civil Rights, 1945–1975.* New York: Vintage, 2006.

Webb, Clive. *Massive Resistance: Southern Opposition to the Second Reconstruction.* New York: Oxford University Press, 2005.

Since 1970

Applebome, Peter. *Dixie Rising: How the South Is Shaping American Values, Politics, and Culture.* San Diego, CA: Harcourt Brace, 1997.

Black, Earl, and Merle Black. *The Rise of Southern Republicans.* Cambridge, MA: Belknap Press for Harvard University Press, 2002.

Cobb, James C., and William W. Stueck, eds. *Globalization and the American South.* Athens: University of Georgia Press, 2005.

Crespino, Joseph A. *In Search of Another Country: Mississippi and the Conservative Counterrevolution.* Princeton, NJ: Princeton University Press, 2007.

Feldman, Glen. *Politics and Religion in the White South.* Lexington: University Press of Kentucky, 2005.

Goldfield, David R. *Black, White, and Southern: Race Relations and Southern Culture, 1940 to the Present.* Baton Rouge: Louisiana State University Press, 1991.

Sale, Kirkpatrick. *Power Shift: The Rise of the Southern Rim and Its Challenge to the Eastern Establishment*. New York: Random House, 1975.

Literature

Andrews, William L., Frances Smith Foster, and Trudier Harris, eds. *The Oxford Companion to African-American Literature*. New York: Oxford University Press, 1997.

Bone, Martyn. *The Postsouthern Sense of Place in Contemporary Fiction*. Baton Rouge: Louisiana State University Press, 2005.

Duck, Leigh Anne. *The Nation's Region: Southern Modernism, Segregation, and U.S. Nationalism*. Athens: University of Georgia Press, 2006.

Greeson, Jennifer. *Our South: Geographic Fantasy and the Rise of National Literature*. Cambridge, MA: Harvard University Press, 2010.

Guinn, Matthew. *After Southern Modernism*. Jackson: University Press of Mississippi, 2000.

Harker, Jamie. *The Lesbian South: Feminists, the Women in Print Movement, and the Queer Literary Canon*. Chapel Hill: University of North Carolina Press, 2018.

Jones, Anne Goodwyn. *Tomorrow Is Another Day: The Woman Writer in the South, 1859–1936*. Baton Rouge: Louisiana State University Press, 1995.

King, Richard H. *A Southern Renaissance: The Cultural Awakening of the American South, 1930–1955*. New York: Oxford University Press, 1982.

Kreyling, Michael. *Inventing Southern Literature*. Jackson: University Press of Mississippi, 1998.

Lowe, John Wharton. *Calypso Magnolia: The Crosscurrents of Caribbean and Southern Literature*. Chapel Hill: University of North Carolina Press, 2016.

Monteith, Sharon, ed. *The Cambridge Companion to the Literature of the American South*. New York: Cambridge University Press, 2013.

Richardson, Riche. *Black Masculinity and the U.S. South: From Uncle Tom to Gangsta*. Athens: University of Georgia Press, 2007.

Yaeger, Patricia. *Dirt and Desire: Reconstructing Southern Women's Writing, 1930–1990*. Chicago: University of Chicago Press, 2000.

Music

Bertrand, Michael T. *Race, Rock, and Elvis*. New York: Macmillan, 1985.

Cooke, Mervyn, and David G. Horn, eds. *The Cambridge Companion to Jazz*. New York: Cambridge University Press, 2002.

Giddins, Gary. *Visions of Jazz: The First Century*. New York: Oxford University Press, 1998.

Goff, James R., Jr. *Close Harmony: A History of Southern Gospel*. Chapel Hill: University of North Carolina Press, 2002.

Grem, Darren. "The South's Got Somethin' to Say: Atlanta's Dirty South and the Southernization of Hip-Hop America." *Southern Cultures* 12 (Winter 2006): 55–73.

Guralnick, Peter. *Last Train to Memphis: The Rise of Elvis Presley*. Boston: Little, Brown, 1994.

Guralnick, Peter. *Sweet Soul Music: Rhythm and Blues and the Southern Dream of Freedom*. New York: Harper & Row, 1966.

Lomax, Alan. *The Land Where the Blues Began*. New York: Dell, 1993.

Lornell, Kip. *Happy in the Service of the Lord: Afro-American Gospel Quartets in Memphis*. Urbana: University of Illinois Press, 1988.

Malone, Bill C. *Country Music, USA*. Austin: University of Texas Press, 2002.

Wald, Elijah. *Escaping the Delta: Robert Johnson and the Invention of the Blues*. New York: Amistad Press, 2005.

Food

Cooley, Angela Jill. *To Live and Dine in Dixie: The Evolution of Urban Food Culture in the Jim Crow South*. Athens: University of Georgia Press, 2015.

Edge, John T. *Potlikker: A Food History of the Modern South*. New York: Penguin Press, 2017.

Egerton, John. *Southern Food: At Home, on the Road, in History*. New York: Alfred A. Knopf, 1987.

Engelhardt, Elizabeth. *A Mess of Greens: Southern Gender and Southern Food*. Athens: University of Georgia Press, 2011.

Ferris, Marcie Cohen. *The Edible South: The Power of Food and the Making of an American Region*. Chapel Hill: University of North Carolina Press, 2014.

Gutierrez, Sandra A. *The New Southern–Latino Table*. Chapel Hill: University of North Carolina Press, 2011.

Harris, Jessica B. *High on the Hog: A Culinary Journey from Africa to America*. New York: Bloomsbury, 2011.

Hilliard, Sam B. *Hog Meat and Hoecake: Food Supply in the Old South, 1840–1860*. Athens: University of Georgia Press, paperback ed. 2014. First published 1972.

Ownby, Ted. *American Dreams in Mississippi: Consumers, Poverty, and Culture, 1830–1898*. Chapel Hill: University of North Carolina Press, 1999.

Taylor, Joe Gray. *Eating, Drinking, and Visiting in the South: An Informal History*. Baton Rouge: Louisiana State University Press, 1982.

Further reading

Index